A LIFE ON THE OCEAN WAVE
AND ON THE SHORE

A Life on the Ocean Wave and on the Shore

by

Peter A. Embley

Scotforth Books, 2002

Copyright © Peter Embley, 2002

First published in 2002 on behalf of the author
by Scotforth Books,
Carnegie House,
Chatsworth Road,
Lancaster LA1 4SL,
England
Tel: +44(0)1524 840111
Fax: +44(0)1524 840222
email: carnegie@provider.co.uk
Publishing and book sales: www.carnegiepub.co.uk
Book production: www.wooof.net

British Library Cataloguing-in-Publication data
A catalogue record for this book is available
from the British Library

ISBN 1-904244-16-5

Typeset by
George Wishart & Associates, Whitley Bay
Printed and bound in the UK by
Bookcraft (Bath) Ltd

Dedication

*To my wife Margaret and her daughter
Linda, who have read my book and
have given me much encouragement.
To Lynne my lovely daughter-in-law,
who did most of my typing on her
computer.*

Contents

vii

CHAPTER I

My Schooldays

We lived close to the Lake District, at Lake Ullswater, and it was there that I remember most from my childhood. The local schools were not very good, or perhaps it was just that I could not fully understand what was required of me. My friend's fathers were either farmers or farm labourers, so I was an outsider. I was different from my friends.

My father was a Sea Captain in the Merchant Navy. In 1941, he had been awarded the OBE (Order of the British Empire) when his ship was torpedoed in the Atlantic. I was told by my mother that father had attempted to save a young boy's life when their lifeboat had been cut in two by a British Destroyer, which had not seen them. My father had also sung to the men in the lifeboat to ensure that they all kept their spirits up. My father had been Chief Officer, and it was one of his officers who had spoke up for him, hence the OBE.

My mother was a remarkable woman, but she was widowed early. I remember vividly the day she learnt that my father was missing. His ship, as had been reported in the *Newcastle Journal*, had hit a mine off the coast of Italy. I was with my mother in the village telephone boxes whilst she endeavoured to obtain confirmation of him and of his ship. I was ten years old; it was 1945 and the war with Japan had just ended. I was not allowed to talk on the telephone, but as soon as mother burst into tears, I knew that my father had, more than likely, drowned. Even one so young can quickly learn the signs of tragedy.

The house was very quiet that night, except for the sound of my mother weeping. It was obvious that she was upset. I felt for my mother, but being so young, I was unable to offer much comfort except to embrace her. She quickly recovered and thought of me and went to see her friend in the village. Two weeks later my mother's friend suggested that she perhaps might try sending me to a Merchant Navy Officers boarding school in Berkshire that she heard was excellent. After much writing and talking on the telephone, my mother asked me that if the school was willing to accept me, would I want to go? I thought that it would be a big adventure going to a boarding school, much better than the local village schools. My sister, Pamela, was about four years older than I, but unfortunately had severe disabilities: she was wheelchair bound, unable to walk or talk properly. Looking back, I can understand the difficulties that my mother must have had preparing me for school, as well as having the responsibility of looking after Pamela.

All the arrangements were eventually completed and a friend was booked to look after Pamela. It took two days by taxis and by train to get to London, where we were eventually met and shown the way, via Waterloo Station, to Winersh Halt Station in Berkshire. We got a taxi to the school from the station, where my adventure was about to start.

I was totally amazed by the sheer size of the school. It looked like a large mansion. We were met by many people, secretaries, masters, and so on, and then shown around. After the introductions had been completed, the school rules were explained to my mother and myself very clearly. The uniform that all the boys had to wear was also presented: grey shirt, short grey trousers, grey socks and black shoes. The school was an orphanage and pupils were only allowed to attend if their father had died in the Merchant Navy. It was explained to us that the uniform would be provided free by the school and must be taken care of at all times. I remember that tears were in my mother's eyes as one of the staff indicated that she should make her goodbyes. She stooped down and whispered to me that she would not be able to come down and see me during term time, which meant that the next time I would be seeing her would be at half-term or the end of the term. I tried to be brave and told my mother not to worry and that I would miss her dearly. Mother told me to telephone if I had any problems or anxieties. I promised her that I would. At my young age, for I was eleven, I knew that my mother had only a widow's pension to survive on and could not afford to travel that often to Berkshire.

Life at the school was new to me and I was regarded by everyone as the new boy. As I lived in a small village, many of the boys used to make jokes at my expense, often referring to me as the village yokel. They would laugh at my speech, often taunting me, but one learns quickly – well, I did anyway. When the boys discovered that their taunts were being ignored, they would go and look for another innocent victim.

After being at my boarding school for about nine months, for I was then about twelve, I then moved up to the seniors. I was chosen by the Commodore (head boy) to become his 'fag' or skivvy. I had to make his bed and keep all his clothes

Royal Merchant School, Bearwood, Wokingham, Berkshire.

and articles tidy. On one particular day whilst I was making his bed, I noticed that one of his sheets was stitched down the centre. Unfortunately, some of the senior boys sharing the same dormitory were watching me make the Commodore's bed. I heard them laughing and then a few of them grabbed hold of me. I was powerless to move and could only watch while they tore the stitching off the sheet that I had been putting on the Commodore's bed. Then they made me make up the bed with the freshly torn sheet ensuring that on the outside the bed looked perfect. That night after the lights out order had been given, the Commodore returned with the Head Girl from a special outing. I heard a bellow, then someone shouting my name. I immediately recognised the Commodore's voice summoning me. I belted down the corridor to the seniors' dormitory. I had to suppress my laughter as the Commodore, although only about sixteen or seventeen, was indeed incredibly tall. He had the torn sheet enveloping his body with only his head visible, sticking through the top. He said, 'Come here boy', and beckoned me with his finger. He then asked, 'Did you make this bed, with this sheet?' After admitting responsibility, he swiftly whacked me in the face with his fist. I went down and stayed down. I was learning fast. I could hear all the senior boys shouting and cheering, this giving me the opportunity to escape without being noticed. In those days the school's discipline was maintained by the senior boy prefects and the house captains.

The school had four Houses in my time: Drake, Frobisher, Hawkins and Raleigh. I was allocated to Drake. There were many competitions, mainly in sport, as the school had five hundred acres of grounds, including a magnificent lake. I found early on that I was good at running and won the mile race two years in succession. I was disappointed not to win it the third year, but I had fractured my ankle playing cricket and had to have my leg put in plaster at Reading Hospital. When the plaster was eventually removed, despite advice not to compete, I did try. My leg was too weak and I fell flat on my face.

The previous year I had been entered into the England Boys' County Championship held at Reading sports stadium. The other boys competing all had the correct footwear, and I had to make do with flimsy plimsolls. I was extremely disappointed to be placed sixth, although I had not trained enough for the race.

By the time I was sixteen, I had risen to become House Captain, but by this time the disciplining procedure had been restricted, which would have pleased me more if I were still a

Visiting dignitaries and the headmaster at the Royal Merchant School inspecting members of Raleigh House, of which I was House Captain (centre right).

junior. The general topic of conversation between my contemporaries was about the things we would do once we had left school. It was commonplace to want to join the Merchant Navy.

When I left the Royal Merchant Navy School, I was given a place at the King Edward the Seventh Nautical College in the East End of London. One of the senior masters had written to the college requesting that I be given a place. My recollection of that period was of catching the Underground from our digs in Kensington to Stepney in East London. I was in awe of the amount of people crowded on to the train each morning. I often wondered whether people's umbrellas would be still sticking out of the doors or into other people for that matter. My studies at the college were about navigation, shipping cargo and ship stability. Towards the end of the three months' training, talk was of which shipping line one would be joining, for we all had different opinions of which to choose. What we all knew, however, was that we would all be off to sea.

CHAPTER II

Off to Sea

It was my mother who helped me with my choice of shipping line by suggesting that I visit my auntie in Crosby, Liverpool. After agreeing to go, all the arrangements were made. I was taken on board several ships at Liverpool docks. I can vividly remember the smell of animal hides being loaded, a distinct smell of which I have not had the pleasure of smelling again. Many suggestions were made about which shipping line was the best, but in fact, I chose a line that had ships regularly sailing from Liverpool. With a lot of help from my aunts, uncles and, of course, my mother, I wrote and was accepted by one of the largest shipping companies in Liverpool, the Ellerman Hall Line. I remember my interview at their head office, at Tower Buildings in Liverpool. It was explained to me that a letter would be sent to my home address with details of my joining instructions. In the office one of the secretaries told me that the Ellerman Hall Line had over two hundred ships, so it was therefore unlikely that I would sail on the same ship twice.

My eagerly awaited letter finally arrived. Naturally, I tore it open. My mother was by my side and as I read it so did she. I was to join the *City of Bedford* at Birkenhead West float dock on the 14 December 1951. As I leapt around the house shouting, my mother quietly reminded me that I had a lot of important things left to do. Getting my uniform and clothes ready was essential, but I also needed a new passport and seaman's discharge book. My mother had saved a small amount of money, but she asked my aunt and uncle in Liverpool if they could help us buy the uniform. Therefore, it was when I was packed and on the train set for Liverpool that I began to realise that my adult life was about to begin.

At my aunt and uncle's house life was hectic. We had to travel into Liverpool city centre to purchase my new apprentice officer's uniform and visit the passport photographer to get my picture taken. This was all novel for me. I needed help and my relations gave it to me in great armfuls. On 11 December I got my first seaman's discharge book and, with my new uniform, was ready to join my first ship in Birkenhead.

CHAPTER III

City of Bedford

J oining a ship can be for anyone a difficult affair, but for me
it was very exciting and, in hindsight, yes, it was difficult.
It was a relatively new ship, and the cargo – bound for India –
was almost loaded. I was quickly introduced to all my new
crewmates who became friends for a short time. The hardest
part was learning all about the new ship. The throb of the
engines disturbed me at first, but it is amazing how one gets
used to the noise.

I had my first taste of seasickness going through the Bay of
Biscay; the ship rolled in the waves. The other apprentices
sympathised with me, but they also told me that the sea was
quite calm at that time. The swell was normally caused by
storms occurring several miles out in the Atlantic, and the
Bay of Biscay had a notorious reputation, which it lived up
to. Mac, the senior apprentice, told me that once we hit the
Mediterranean the swell would disappear and things would
calm down. He had been on the bridge and had peeked at the
current chart so he knew the ship's position.

As an apprentice, I quickly learnt that we had many duties
to perform such as keeping watch on the bridge with one of
the senior officers on his tour of duty.

We soon reached the Suez Canal, and the canal pilot knew
every inch of the water and advised the Captain which
course to steer to guide us through. The next port of call was

at Aden, where we took aboard fresh supplies of water, stores and oil fuel for the engines. It was extremely hot there compared with the weather in Britain. However, we were there for less than a day before moving off to sea again. We steamed through the Indian Ocean for a long time, then docked in Karachi in Pakistan, where we discharged some of the cargo. A day later we were steaming down the Indian coast towards my first sight of Bombay. The docks of Bombay were almost full of ships of different types, bulk ore carriers and tankers, and of many different nationalities.

It was a couple of hours later when I went with Mac to view the city. Walking through the dock gate, I was truly amazed at the sight that greeted us. There were crowds of people with market stalls everywhere. There was a policeman on the street trying to move people on to the side to allow cars and buses to pass by. The smells and sounds of the people selling their products and arguing loudly truly astounded me. My friend was laughing at me, pulling me along. The women were wearing lovely long skirts; I was told that they were called saris. They chose bright colours for festive events, which could and did include mundane activities such as shopping and conversing with friends. I was fascinated; I had never seen anything like this before. I suddenly felt a tug on my sleeve and when I looked round there was a group of young boys calling to me. 'Rupee mister please.' I fished in my pocket but found that the crowd of boys was running after coins that Mac had thrown onto the floor. He was laughing at the boys, who were pushing and shoving each other to get the money. He explained that I would have to be extra careful as there were many pickpockets about. I now understood the terrible poverty that some people of India had got accustomed to.

We walked quickly, Mac guiding me along to the post office, which as everywhere else was crowded. I bought some stamps so I could post my letters back home. Mac said to me as we were leaving the post office, 'You seem to be enjoying yourself', but after a while it just became a normal event. The bodies of men and women were curled up in their saris sleeping in any place they could find, on and under benches, on concrete floors – you really had to watch where you stepped. My companion decided that we should be getting back to the ship.

The next day Mac told me that he wanted to show me what cargo we were loading and how to ensure that it was stowed well. We had to change to go down the cargo hatches into the cargo holds. The noise from the steam cargo winches was deafening. The cargo derricks were up and cargo was being loaded into the holds. Heavy packing boxes coming from England were being taken out of the holds and lowered ashore. Bales of a yellow substance – I was informed that it was jute – were being hoisted by the winches from the dock quay and loaded in the ship's hold. The Indian dock workers manoeuvred these bales. Mac asked me to climb down the hold ladder, being careful to watch for the derrick loading the bales of jute into the hold with a large iron stop. I found it was a long way down and had to hold on tightly with my heavy leather gloves. Mac was much quicker than I was, and even though I had tried to be quick, I had a lot to learn about using iron ladders. Climbing down the ladder with such a huge drop was daunting, but I had to get the knack of using the hold ladders. The air in the hold was much cooler than it had been on the deck. I watched as Mac explained what we were to do down there. He motioned me to move to the starboard side and to get the Indian dockers to move the bales into more even rows. After much deliberation with the headman, they began to do this. We then went up the ladders to the next few holds, which by this time were almost completely discharged.

The following day, Sunday, Mac suggested that as the dock workers had the day off, it would be a shame if we did not go anywhere. He suggested that it would be nice to visit Beach Kandy Swimming Pool, as he said it was for Europeans only. I was delighted and joined a party of Navigating Officers and engineers who also had the day free and who also wanted to go swimming. Beach Kandy was lovely, although not a beach at all but a circular swimming area with a raft in the centre and grass around the edges. We had a marvellous day, the best day I had had since being on ship. I can remember swimming to the centre of the pool and diving off the raft into the cool water. We naturally played around, and as I was the youngest I seemed to receive the best treatment from the other officers and engineers, much unlike my school days. Time flew by, and before I knew it, Mac was indicating that it was time to get changed and get ready to return to the ship. I noticed in one of the mirrors that my thin body was becoming a shade of pink from the scorching sun. I knew that I would have to be careful as sun cream was one item I did not possess. We headed for the transport that was taking us back to the ship. I became aware that I had met so many more crewmembers in this one afternoon than I had on the actual ship. I was very sorry to be leaving Beach Kandy as I had enjoyed myself, but as I was told and later found out for myself, this would be the first of many good times at Beach Kandy.

Back on board ship, the routine of discharging our British cargo was almost completed and the loading of the Indian cargo – raw materials like jute, sisal and tea chests – was beginning. I was back on duty, going up and down cargo hatches, which by now was merely a routine, ensuring the dockers were loading the cargo correctly. The Second Officer, with guidance from the first officer, was supervising everything. Therefore, it was our duty to report to the senior officers anything that wasn't being done properly. Loading was completed by the sixth day, after much hard work by the multitude of dock workers. While we had been in port, the Chief Officer had also been supervising the army of Indian maintenance workers who were hanging over the side of the ship, chipping off rust areas and painting over the patches. We were getting ready to leave Bombay, our pilot was coming aboard to guide us out of harbour and I could hear our engines steaming up. Our ship whistle was sounding and shouts from the bridge were also clearly heard. 'Let go forward.' This instructed the workers on the dock to let go of the mooring ropes that were secured to the dock bollards.

We were soon moving astern, the sea churning up behind us as the propeller bit into the water. We were now off towards home. Our first port of call would be Aden, then Port Suez, Avonmouth near Bristol before finally reaching my longed for destination, Liverpool. My duties were now on ship watches with the Chief Officer on the 4 a.m. to 8 a.m. watch and the same in the evening. Being a junior apprentice meant that I had to be on duty with the Chief Officer. I was told to treat him circumspectly, always addressing him as 'Sir'. It was understood that if I did not respect him and carry out my duties, then there would be a price to pay. I worked hard and ensured that my duties were carried out conscientiously. This paid off and one day when everything was quiet, he took me onto the bridge. The horizon was clear, and the Chief Officer showed me all the pieces of equipment that were used to guide the ship. The echo sounder, which is used in narrow water channels to tell the officers the depth of the water, and the radar, which detects any other ships or obstructions, and the coastline, which showed up as a white line on the screen. He explained everything to me and then passed me a pair of binoculars. I was in awe and felt extremely privileged. I found using the telescope the most difficult, but as the senior officer explained, it was only really used to magnify an image that needed scrutinising, like seeing the name on the side of a ship passing by. He then showed me the ship's logbook, where all the main events were recorded. Each British ship had to carry a logbook, which the Captain ensured was kept up to date.

I was in awe of the wonderful sights of the porpoises leaping gracefully out of the sea time and again – it was magnificent. We also witnessed several small water spouts that seemed to come from nowhere.

Aden was now in sight, we had steamed right across the Indian Ocean. The tranquillity had now disappeared: the guidance pilot climbed aboard from the launch and up the rope ladder and the engine room telegraph clanged continuously. Everyone was moving. We had to manoeuvre to drop anchor.

Within minutes, the sea was alive with small boats coming towards us to trade their wares. It was a free trade port with no duty to pay on the goods bought. Many of us looked around for any bargains. There were Rolex lighters, gold watches, cameras, perfume, and so on. Mac told me to watch what I was buying before I gave away my money. He told me he would help me look for some bargains. I thanked him, but when I turned around, he had already moved off.

Time passed quickly and before I knew we were steaming out of Aden and heading up the Red Sea for Port Suez. We anchored briefly in the bitter lakes, halfway through the Suez Canal. Someone told me that they were called the bitter lakes because they were extremely salty and therefore much more buoyant than normal seawater. We were soon dropping off the Suez Canal pilot and moving out into the Mediterranean for the last leg of the voyage home.

The last part of the voyage went quickly and everyone was busy ensuring that their clothes were spotlessly clean and ready for packing. Wives and girlfriends were finally going to see their men, and don't forget my dear mum! I soon learnt that our schedule had been revised. We were now going directly to Tilbury in Essex, not Avonmouth or even Liverpool. There were many groans of discontent when the news eventually filtered around the ship, but homeward bound to England at least. Train tickets would have to be bought. Most people would head via London to their final destination. I, like many others, headed for the post office to send a telegram to my mother to let her know where we were docking and when I would eventually be arriving home. I did so after a very long journey north via London and on to Penrith in Cumberland (now Cumbria). I had to walk with my suitcase and wait at the bus station for the bus to the nearest village to my home. I arrived home at last, and as my mother said, 'the wanderer returns'; it was just marvellous to be home again.

CHAPTER IV

Home for the First Time

The next day was tiresome as my mother wanted to know every aspect of my voyage and every detail of the ship. As my father had been a Captain in the Merchant Navy, mother had been on several of his ships. She was quite incredulous of the changes in modern ships in the 1950s. I had to explain everything over and over; so many times in fact that it seemed like *Twenty Questions* off the television. I drank many cups of tea and got lots of hugs and kisses. Many of mother's friends called in to see us that day and mother had to try and recall what I had told her about my first voyage. My sister Pamela was wheeled in to join us and looked at me quite animatedly and gave me a hard squeeze to let me know how much she cared for me. It was a moment that I failed to thank everyone for because it was so special that I was almost struck dumb with emotion with all the interest, handshakes and my sister's hugs. My own friends, Eric and his brother, came in to hear part of my story and wanted to know whether I had seen a whale and which of the places I had visited I had liked best.

As our house was very close to Lake Ullswater, my friends wanted me to go with them to get a boat out on the lake. I think they wanted to know how much my rowing had improved. However, once they noticed that there was little change, I had to explain that working on a large cargo ship was different from being in a small rowing boat. They soon lost interest, which pleased me. One of my friends had a small fishing line and we took turns trying to catch fish. The days at home soon sped by and as my four weeks' leave was almost at an end, a letter from the company arrived. Before I could read it mother was by my side and read out aloud: 'You are to join the ship *City of Leicester* in Liverpool.' 'We must try and get your clothes washed, dried and ironed by the sixteenth – that's only a week away! Go on now, get all your dirty clothes together and bring down any shirts that need buttons sewing on. Don't forget your shoes need a good polish and your uniform needs brushing and pressing. We must make sure that we have sufficient hot water for you to get a bath and don't forget your ears need a good wash and clean.' From past experiences, I knew that mother would ignore any protest, so I decided to get on with doing what she had asked. With shoes cleaned, uniform pressed and a hot bath completed – with mother coming into the bathroom to wash behind my ears! – I headed for Penrith Station. I would then commute to Liverpool Lime Street Station, where I would be joining the *City of Leicester* in Birkenhead. To save money, I got a taxi to the Liverpool Pier head and caught the Mersey Ferry to Birkenhead. It was a novelty for me, seeing the Liver Building's clock faces from the river, a familiar sight for all Liverpudlians. I then caught a cab on the other side and headed for my ship. The taxi driver had to stop his cab at the entrance gate as the gateman wanted to see my discharge book. 'Joining that old tub up there, are you?' I just nodded, and the taxi continued through the gates. I recognised instantly the familiar colours of the city ships' funnels: buff white and black.

My second adventure was about to begin.

CHAPTER V

City of Leicester

On introduction to the other apprentice officers, I was informed that the ship had three days left in Birkenhead before sailing to Antwerp in Belgium. We only spent a few days in Antwerp before heading back to complete the loading of industrial goods in Birkenhead due for Pakistan and India. The industrial goods included a locomotive and heavy lifts, which needed to be anchored with wire hawsers to ensure that they would not move. However, the Liverpool dockers knew their job well and no instruction from any crew members was needed because all the goods were well secured. The ship was quite old, built c.1925, much older than the first ship that I had sailed on, and was powered by coal. This was more of a job for the boiler men whom I am sure would have much preferred to be working on a ship powered by oil and diesel. Our speed only reached ten and a half knots, about twelve miles an hour. It was going to be a long journey to Bombay. The Chief Officer put me on watch on the bridge, which meant less sleep, four hours on, four hours off. It was just as well that the Chief Officer put me on day work when we got through the Bay of Biscay for I had time to catch up on some sleep. I was given maintenance work with a fellow apprentice, John, cleaning the brass work in the wheel-house.

It took a week to get through the Mediterranean to Port

Suez. The coal made the funnels belch out black smoke into the still air. We called briefly at Aden, taking on fresh water and stores and then we headed for Bombay. It was now mid-May 1952, the air was hot and clammy and I was glad I had chosen a navigation profession and not an engineering one. A week later we took on our Bombay pilot, who guided us into the Alexander Dock in Bombay harbour. The pattern of the previous voyage was continued. We discharged our English cargo, which took six days.

We then set off north heading for Karachi in Pakistan. We were docked in Karachi longer this time as there was more cargo to unload. Bales of hemp and jute were loaded as well as coal. This was a very unusual sight for me. Pakistani women with old, tatty sarongs carrying baskets of coal on their heads were shuffling along in a snake line, flinging their loads down into chutes. The coal dust settled everywhere, but mostly on the women. I was curious about the weight of the baskets they carried and beckoned one of the women over to me. The weight was unbelievable and as to how they carried the baskets on their heads, I will never know. Suddenly, there was a deafening shout and I turned to see the Chief Officer beckoning me. After explaining what I was doing, he promptly replied, 'Your curiosity may land you in serious difficulties.' Therefore, I carried on with my work, supervising the loading of the cargo. It was quite a physical job, up and down steel ladders into the cargo holds, but one where time seemed to pass by quickly.

The next day we left Karachi and headed for Bedi Bunda, a day's sailing. We had to drop anchor as there was no quay, but we only planned to be there for two days. The Chief Officer put both John and I on anchor watch. The ship was loading bales of wool and cotton, using our own derricks and steam winches, which were very noisy. We had to keep a check on our position every fifteen minutes to ensure that the ship was not moving or 'dragging the anchor'. This broke the mundane routine, which we were both pleased about.

After the planned two days in Bedi Bunda, we weighed anchor for Port Sudan in the Red Sea. It was stiflingly hot in Port Sudan loading bales of cotton with sweat pouring off us as we climbed up and down the steel ladders. The steel walls of the cargo holds were very hot, so we had to wear protective gloves to prevent our hands being burnt, but the gloves only encouraged our hands to sweat more.

It was not long before we were sailing through the Suez Canal and I was looking forward to going for a swim in the bitter lakes. In two weeks' time we would be back in sweet England, a thought that kept me going.

On arriving in England, we went to Avonmouth first to discharge some raw materials before docking in Liverpool. I was to be home for four weeks. The ship was then headed up to Glasgow, to the breaker's yard to be broken up for scrap metal. We were on the ship's last voyage, which was a sad occasion. It was now packing time for most of us, and being mid-August, the weather would be pleasant for all those travelling home.

CHAPTER VI

City of Swansea

While at home a letter arrived telling me to join my third ship, the *City of Swansea*. I was to join her in Liverpool, a city that I was becoming very familiar with. I joined on a Tuesday and met my colleague, Laurie, the other apprentice with whom I would be working with for the following four weeks. This was to be a special voyage for me as it was a voyage around the world. First to America, then to the Philippines, Hong Kong, Singapore and then to Japan. Our first port of call would be Montreal in Canada. The ship carried passengers as well as cargo, and we were told to look smart at all times, shoes shining and uniform brushed. However, we had to work as normal. There was plenty to see this time as we crossed the Atlantic and picked up our St Laurence pilot. I was fascinated at the white houses on the banks of the mighty river; it was just like something out of a film. Laurie told me that in the winter months the St Lawrence was closed because it all iced up, so going to Canada in the winter meant going to Halifax in Nova Scotia.

We stayed in Montreal for slightly more than a week. We managed to get ashore a few times and on one of our visits, Laurie decided to go sight seeing. We were told not to miss a visit to Mount Royal. We took the advice and after a long climb, it was definitely worth it. It was a truly memorable time. We could see the entire city spread out below us: the

Having a drink with a colleague in a New York bar.

St Lawrence River, McGill University, the horse-drawn carriages and the park, which had squirrels scampering about everywhere. I was glad that I had brought my camera with me. We could see Notre Dame Church and the Jacques Cartier Bridge over the river. Checking our dollars, we decided to take the tram on a sightseeing tour of the city. It is a city that I shall never forget.

Sailing time was approaching, however. We passed the heights of Quebec, a place famous for people attempting to scale it, and were now sailing for the Delaware River up to Philadelphia. We were only there for a day before steaming off for New York. We docked in Brooklyn for three days and then headed south, first calling at Newport News and then carrying on further south to the West Indies. We had to take on more fuel at Curaco before beginning our stretch down to the Panama Canal.

24

Once through the canal, we had to steam north for Long Beach, California, a navy port in Los Angeles and then up to San Francisco. We managed to reach San Francisco even though the fog was so dense that it was impossible to view any of the city or its surroundings. We then steamed down the southern Pacific to Manila in the Philippines, a long journey taking more than two weeks. Our ship had to anchor in the bay, so barges had to travel out to us, before travelling to a smaller, less well-known port, Cebu. After spending a day there, we left and headed for Hong Kong. It was by now mid-November, but the harbour was very crowded. We travelled to ports in Japan: Kobe, Hironhata, Nagoya, Shimbinizu and Yokohama. I bought a tea set off a barge in Nagoya from a Japanese woman, and to this day, more than forty years later, it is still almost intact.

We then steamed northwards to a port called Otaru. It was snowing heavily and was extremely cold, about sixteen degrees Fahrenheit. Loading the timber was a dangerous ordeal as it was difficult keeping one's feet from slipping on the steel deck and ladders, but as one of my colleagues warned me, the contrasts in temperature were just a part of the job.

Our return journey to England started from the port of Moji, via Hong Kong, where we had to load heavy tanks. One of the tanks, a Churchill, weighed forty tons, which meant that the lifting crane had to be used. We spent our Christmas in Singapore and we made it ashore to sample some of the delights of the city. We returned home, via Malaya, Port Swetenham, Penang and Columbo in Sri Lanka, and then through the Suez Canal. It was now mid-January 1953. Our next port of call was Algiers, before steaming up the Thames to berth at Tilbury.

It had been some voyage, seeing so many new and exciting countries and ports, but now it was time to pack and prepare to go on leave. I had met many new faces, some of which were now friends. Leaving the ship sent many different emotions through me all at the same time. It was now once again time to work out how to get home. As it turned out, many of us going on leave were heading for London, so I was able to join some of my colleagues. I had to find a post office so I could send a telegraph to my mother telling her when to expect me home. Next, I was at the ticket information desk to enquire about the train timetables. All went well and I was soon seated on the train wishing that the eight hours travel would pass quickly.

I was received with warm greetings from both my mother and Pamela, and I was quick telling them that my voyage had been a long one, so it might be better to wait till the morning to hear any story telling. Reluctantly they both agreed, meaning I could now relax and enjoy a good night's sleep. I reflected, before dropping off to sleep, on the wonderful journey I had just experienced.

The next day and for the following several days my tale was related to my mother's friends over and over again. It was now the middle of winter and bleak clouds and rain prevented me from helping with any jobs outside.

CHAPTER VII

City of Yokohama

My next letter soon arrived, which meant that the next couple of days would pass in a busy whirl. I was to join the *City of Yokohama* in Birkenhead on the following Monday. News in my small village travelled quickly and this time on my departure there were many people waving me goodbye. I was disappointed when I first saw the ship. It was a mess. She was still undergoing repairs and was already loading cargo. I met Dave Russell, another apprentice, who would be my colleague for the voyage. We shared a cabin and were told that we would be heading to East Africa. Our first port of call after the Suez Canal and Aden would be Mombassa, and I can tell you I was really looking forward to feeling the sun on my back. I got to know Dave well and after exchanging our life stories I learnt that he had been on more voyages that me, so technically he was my senior.

The ship was old, built in 1918, but it burnt oil, which was useful because it is quicker to take on oil as fuel than coal is. We would be leaving Birkenhead the following day, but before commencing the journey, we had to calibrate our direction finder. We had a compass adjuster to check that our compass was accurate. It all went to plan and we commenced our journey on Thursday, 5 March 1953. We dropped our pilot off at Holyhead and headed south for the Mediterranean. The repairs to the engines were completed and the

27

City of Yokohama leaving Calcutta, India.

engineers left the ship at the same time as the pilot. Dave and I were given watch work for the first day and a half by our Chief Officer, Paddy O'Driscoll. He then transferred us to day work, cleaning and ensuring that the ship was tidy at all times.

We were due to arrive in our first African port, Mombassa, on my birthday, but as you can imagine, nothing stopped our schedule. We docked in Mombassa harbour and our winches and heavy lift cranes were soon busy. We had many army vehicles and stores to discharge, and once this was done our priorities lessened. We were moved out of the dock and back to the anchorage, which meant that Dave and I were given anchor watch for the next week. It can be very boring looking at the same scene all the time. The routine became second nature but we had to be reasonably alert as the officers would creep around corners ensuring that we had not fallen asleep. Dave told me that we were going into Mombassa to complete our discharge of UK cargo before moving down to Dares-Salaam, Zanzibar and Tango to load oil cake hides and sisal.

We were now heading home by way of Aden to take on more fuel and stores and spent Coronation Day, 2 June, at sea with a small ceremony on the fore deck.

It was mid-summer and we had to anchor in the bitter lakes for two hours – just enough time for a quick swim. Dave and I swam around the ship. He was quicker than I and was near the gangway when the Chief Officer's sharp whistle blast signalled us to get out and dry. I was still only half way round the ship and had to rush to get out. I was out of breath and Dave had to haul me out of the lake. We quickly dried ourselves and were soon on duty again.

We stopped briefly in Port Said to take on more fresh water and fuel oil and then continued on our voyage home through the Mediterranean, which, despite our full speed, eleven and a half knots, took forever. The first English home port was Avonmouth before the ship returned to Liverpool. Dave and I were very keen to return home, he to meet his girlfriend and I to meet my mother and Pamela. I thought of how nice it would be to have a girlfriend of my own. The weather was glorious, the sun beating down on us in this glorious month of June. This was going to be an enjoyable leave. The greetings were warming accompanied by endless questions.

I spent the next weeks enjoying long bike rides. One particular afternoon we rode up the Kirkstone Pass, a difficult and tiring ride, and then cycled to Glenridding before catching the Ullswater ferry to Howtown. The ferry trip had saved us several more miles cycling. We only had three miles left to ride once we had got off the ferry to reach home. A message by letter had arrived that day instructing me to rejoin the *City of Yokohama* in Glasgow. It would be my fifth voyage, this one being on the same vessel that I had only left four weeks previously.

The ship was exactly the same, except that the crewmembers were no longer the same, even Dave had been replaced by Billy. I had not met Billy before and had much to talk about. It is necessary to be friendly and get to know each other quickly as you have to share a cabin. We spent three days in Glasgow, a city I had not visited before, and Billy agreed to show me around. He showed me all the best places to visit and also the public houses to avoid if one didn't want any trouble. I found from my limited experience that it was easier to get to know a person ashore. This happened to us both as we enjoyed ourselves, drinking a few pints of bitter, strolling around the city and sightseeing. We both knew that we would be moving out the next day to the 'explosive' anchorage, something neither of us was keen on, but we had to just think of it as cargo.

We moved from the bay to the explosive anchorage next morning. I was told to mount the red flag to indicate to other ships that we were loading explosives and to keep clear. We moved down the River Clyde to Greenock, with over two hundred tons of explosives aboard – rockets, gelignite and detonators – heading for Basrah in the Persian Gulf. It would be extremely hot there as it was now nearly the end of July. I hoped, as most of us did, that we would be anchoring in the bitter lakes in the Suez Canal. Sure enough we did, but disappointingly only for an hour, givingthose who were off duty just enough time to have a quick dip.

We departed for Aden to load more water and fuel oil, arriving there in mid-August 1953. Two weeks later we had crossed the sea to the Gulf ports of Basrah Ross Tam Tamara and Mina Al Ahmadi, then up to Basrah, where we had to discharge some of the explosives.

It was exceedingly hot. We were dressed in our tropical clothing, whites and khaki for working on deck supervising the discharge of the cargo with short sleeve shirts, khaki shorts and white socks. We could have cooked fried eggs on the steel deck, it was that hot. We had to ensure at all times that we were wearing gloves when climbing down the ladders into the holds. The Chief Steward insisted that we take salt tablets each day to avoid heat exhaustion as we all sweated so much.

We completed the discharge of cargo and then steamed to Bombay in India to go into dry dock to complete repairs. It took three days to finish the repairs, with gangs of Indians chipping away at the rusted sections. We were then off to Vishakhapatnam to load manganese ore, which often left a thick powder everywhere. I could imagine spending the next few days cleaning the dirt, which abounded everywhere.

I was varnishing the port side cabin of the bridge when the Chief Officer called me over. 'I have a surprise for you young man. You are to transfer over to the *City of Madras* as quickly as possible, so you had better get a move on.' I had to pack all my things and explain to Billy, who was not only my colleague, but also had become a friend, what was happening. He was delighted for me as the ship I would be joining was much newer, but I was not, after all Billy would arrive home well before I would.

CHAPTER VIII

City of Madras

Time flies, it was now January 1954 and I was still in Calcutta, India, although I was now aboard a new ship, the *City of Madras*. The ship was sailing between India and the USA. I was able to see my previous ship, the *City of Yokohama*, come steaming past, belching smoke but homeward bound. A fortnight later we were also leaving, but for another destination, Colombo in Sri Lanka to load tea and cinnamon before heading to Alleppey and Cochin on India's west coast. We stopped briefly in Aden to load oil fuel for our engines, then steamed up the Red Sea to the Suez Canal.

We anchored for an hour in the bitter lakes, but as it was half past midnight, no one felt like a swim. We cleared the Suez Canal by that evening and steamed to Algiers for water and fuel oil.

We then headed off for Boston in mid-February. The skies were heavy and grey and there was heavy swelling, which meant that we were rolling and pitching heavily. The Indian stewards were the most frightened, praying as the ship gave an extra roll with the gale-force winds blowing around us. The swell soon eased off though and everyone seemed in a better mood. We tied up alongside the quay in Boston on Monday, 1 March and commenced the discharge of the cargo.

T.S.S. City of Madras in Boston harbour, Massachusetts, USA.

We were soon proceeding to Baltimore via the Cape Cod Canal, where we picked up our canal pilot who would guide us into Baltimore harbour. We were at anchor there only two days before a message came through for us to head to Newport News and then to Philadelphia. We steamed up the Delaware River and tied up alongside Pier 28 South, where gangs of stevedores began unloading some of the raw materials. Two days later we went up the Hudson River to New York and tied up alongside Pier Number 2.

The docks were deathly silent and we soon found out that the dock workers were on unofficial strike. There was a dispute between two unions, but we, however, managed to get the repairs done to our engines. We were then off to St Johns New Brunswick in Canada, arriving through thick fog to load wood pulp into our holds. The dockers were working

T.S.S. City of Madras shipping water in rough weather.

quickly and it was not long before two thousand seven hundred tons of cargo was loaded aboard. It was now the end of March and we were steaming through the Atlantic heading for the warmer seas of the Mediterranean and then through the Suez Canal and down the Red Sea, halting briefly in Aden to take on more fuel oil and water. Orders then came for all officers and cadets to change into our tropical clothing. The temperature was still rising, and although it was hot, it was not unbearable.

Our next port of call was Karachi in Pakistan where as soon as we arrived and our gangways were lowered, there were lots of men hurrying aboard, removing tarpaulins and hatch covers for every hold. I had been into the city several times before. The next day, after having discharged four hundred tons of general cargo, we were steaming south for

*Fourth Mate Quigley
and me aboard the
T.S.S. City of Madras
waiting to go ashore in
Columbo, Sri Lanka.*

the Manganese port of Cochin and then on to Colombo in
Sri Lanka to load more supplies.

Then north and east to our ship's namesake, Madras, where
we loaded bales of jute. I had never seen much of the city
before, so with a day off I strolled around with a colleague of
mine, of course ending up in a quaint bar, which was mostly
frequented by Anglo-Saxons. We chatted and exchanged
greetings, and it reminded me that I had not been home for
more than nine months.

The next day we loaded five hundred tons of ore and hide
for New York and took on more water and fuel oil in
Colombo. We were now bound for the USA. We had a good

Atlantic crossing, with very little swell, but the temperature did drop to about sixty-five degrees Fahrenheit, so the orders came to change out of our tropical kit and back into blues once more.

We docked in Boston, then a week later headed for New York. This time the dockers were back at work and began discharging the cargo. We had to move to Weehoken to discharge one thousand five hundred tons of manganese ore and then went to our next port at Baltimore with our pilot's guidance.

It was 31 July 1954, and with all the discharge complete, I began experiencing violent pains in my stomach. After an examination by the doctor, I was told that I might be suffering from appendicitis and was promptly taken by ambulance to Baltimore General Hospital. After many questions and further examinations, I was told that I was going to need an operation to remove my appendix. The doctors were very efficient, the operation being carried out smoothly and I was soon resting up in my hospital bed. I became quite friendly with one of the nurses and also with an American patient in the next bed. He always used to call me 'Limey' and would often throw me packets of Lucky Strike cigarettes. I liked Peggy, one of the nurses, and she invited me to her house for a meal. The meal was huge. I was in Baltimore Hospital for eleven days and once the stitches were removed, I was told to travel to New York by train to join up with a Cunard liner, the *Mauretania*.

I was about to become a tourist passenger in the glorious month of August. The ship had a lavish swimming pool, which I was determined to try, despite only having my operation two weeks previously. The water felt divine, and

Postcard of the Cunard R.M.S. Mauretania.

the small scar that now appeared at the bottom of my stomach gave me no pain. It felt like a busman's holiday, and one that I enjoyed immensely. I talked to many of the passengers and entertained them with my tales of lonely voyages and exciting cities.

The days passed quickly. It had now been thirteen months since I had been at sea, that long since I had been home. The liner was now moving into the River Mersey, and I was very excited about the prospect of seeing my mother and sister. I rushed down to my cabin to pack all my clothes, squeezing gently passed a rather large woman, who rather than being embarrassed simply laughed as we extracted ourselves from one another. I thought to myself that it might be worthwhile to stop rushing about so much, but to this day, I have never stopped being active and hasty, despite many warnings.

When I reached the gangway, I felt like royalty, as there was a guard of honour waiting to see all the passengers off. There was a queue of taxis waiting by the ship, so I climbed into one and headed for Lime Street Station. We sped to the station were I purchased a ticket and found the train I needed, which was already waiting on the platform. Almost four hours later I was home, hugging my mother and Pamela. It was delightful to be home again after such a long time away, especially as it was mid-August and the flowers in the garden were in full bloom.

My mother mentioned casually that it would be nice once I had settled in if I could perhaps help out in the garden. The next day I cleaned the lawn mower and set about cutting the grass and then hoeing the edges. The garden was not very large but I was unused to gardening. My mother would appear from time to time with tea and biscuits, smiling as I worked. She was concerned about me overdoing things as I had not long recovered from my operation. After four days of helping around the house and garden I decided to take some time out and enrolled in some dance classes. My mother thought this was very amusing and teased me as she thought I was just after chasing the girls. The dance school, which was opposite the post office, had some vacancies. The team, a lady and gentleman, welcomed me and told me that there would be a class that afternoon. I attended the basic course of dance lessons for the following three weeks before my next letter arrived instructing me to join my next ship, the *City of Coventry*.

My five weeks' leave had passed incredibly quickly and I was soon preparing all my belongings before taking a taxi to Liverpool.

CHAPTER IX

City of Coventry

I joined the *City of Coventry* on Tuesday 28 September. It was relatively new, with a steam turbine engine. It had only just returned from India so the cadet cabin was empty as a few of the crew had gone on leave. I was going that evening to try out my newly found dancing skills at the Atlantic House. It was Saturday night and the local 'scousers' were in good spirits as the football team, Liverpool, had beaten Nottingham County that day. The Reds' fans were delighted and from that evening I became a fellow Red, but my dancing, however, had not improved a great deal.

We were to go up the Manchester Ship Canal to Eastham, moving to Runcorn, passing a ship called the *City of Delhi* and mooring ahead of her. We had more repairs to complete as we had broke several wire straps and had to be towed up the canal. We had to await a berth in Manchester, and when one became free, we continued loading cargo. On completion, we steamed down to Avonmouth as we had to go into dry dock for more repairs. I managed to get weekend leave, which enabled me to spend a couple of days at home with my mother. It was better than nothing.

When I returned to the ship, Gordon Stockdale had joined the crew as a junior apprentice, so I had a new colleague to share the work with and a new person to make friends with.

Time had again flown by, it was now mid-November and

M.V. City of Coventry in Colombo harbour, Sri Lanka.

we were steaming off through the Mediterranean to the Suez Canal. We anchored as usual in the bitter lakes, this time as it was mid-morning those off duty could go swimming for an hour or two. Soon we were heading for Bombay having bunkered for oil and water in Aden. We were only in Bombay for three weeks, long enough for some people, however. Those inclined went for a party at Beach Kandy to do a spot of sunbathing and swimming. We then left Bombay for Karachi, where we spent Christmas Day. There was no cargo work on Christmas Day, but no celebrating either, a quiet drink for the most of us was the limit. Boxing Day was a different story. It was back to work, loading bags of oil cake and one thousand tons of chrome ore.

It was then the start of our journey home by way of Bedi Bunder, again stopping at Aden for supplies. We steamed to Port Sudan, where it was very warm for the usual blustery month of January, and began loading cotton seed, cotton bales and tins of corned beef. We were now fully loaded with one thousand five hundred tons of cargo. We then headed for the Suez Canal – no swim in the bitter lakes this time as we anchored at two in the morning – then through to the Mediterranean leaving the canal behind. When time permitted, I studied hard, hoping to gain my Second Officer's certificate.

Meanwhile, our first port of call at home would be Avonmouth. The docks were full, however, and there was no berth for us, so we had to moor alongside the Bibby Line Ship Motor vessel *Derbyshire*. It was here that I was called up to the Chief Officer's cabin and handed an urgent letter. I opened it with trembling fingers. Had something happened to my mother or to Pamela? My mind twirled with the endless possibilities. The Chief Officer spoke up. 'It's good news son, so open it quickly.' I was to go home for two days and then travel down to Southampton to join the Cunard Liner *Samaria* travelling to New York as acting fourth mate. I was stunned. There was so much to take in from such a small letter. The Chief Officer had a broad grin on his face. 'Told you it was good news. I see that you will soon be joining the officers' ranks, you must have friends in high places.' The goodbyes were to follow, and with my case packed, I took a taxi to Liverpool Lime Street Station.

I was soon home to the mixed feelings of my mother. She was delighted that I was to be promoted but disappointed that I had to leave so soon for London. With my clothes washed, ironed and packed, I was now ready for my new adventure travelling down to London by train. I was told in the letter that I was booked in to the Charing Cross Hotel

Painting deck games on the boat deck.

overnight before I was due to catch the boat train to Southampton.

Once in Southampton, I booked a taxi to take me straight to join the Cunard Liner *Sumaria*. I was a tourist passenger once more. The liner was much smaller and older than my previous passenger liners, but as I was just a passenger, I did not mind.

CHAPTER X

City of New York:
The First and Second Trips

We were soon steaming out into the Atlantic heading for Halifax in Nova Scotia, Canada, where I would be joining the *City of New York*. It was cold being mid-February as I climbed aboard, and I soon found myself being introduced to the officers and taken to my cabin. I found it a great privilege having my own cabin, now that I was Fourth Officer, and I found that my duties were now on the bridge. Snow held up our cargo in St John New Brunswick, but to compensate the Canadian dockers had agreed to work through the night. Our full cargo was complete by the end of the following week, and on 2 March we set sail for India. My cargo duties were much the same as before, supervising any discharge of cargo aboard ship. We steamed through the Mediterranean and through the Suez Canal briefly calling at Aden again for fuel and oil supplies.

We steamed into Bombay at the end of March with nearly one thousand tons of cargo to discharge. The cargo work went well without any problems and before long we were in Cochin in south-west India arriving two days after my birthday. We continued to discharge the cargo before steaming down to Colombo, Sri Lanka, where we found that there was no berth for us to anchor. We therefore had to anchor in Colombo Bay, discharging our

City of New York.

cargo into small barges. Although the dockers worked extremely hard, we found that there was a shortage of
barges.

On 16 April we headed for Madras on the east coast of
India, then up to Chittagong in Bangladesh, where we had to
load jute and complete our discharge of paper pulp. It was
almost the celebration of Ramadam at that time and the
Chief Serang had made a special curry for all the officers,
standing in front of us all with arms folded as the steward
served us this delightful treat. To this day, when there is even
the faintest hint of curry aroma in the air, I am reminded
clearly of that event. It certainly turned out to be a special
curry and an extremely hot one at that! Everyone seemed to
drink gallons of water to help the meal down as the Serang
stayed in the saloon until everyone's plate was cleared. My

eyes watered for days after that meal, even at the thought of the curry.

We steamed round to Calcutta with the help of a pilot guiding us through the Hougli River were we completed the loading round the clock. Our Second and Third Officers were being relieved that week, so we had new officers to get to know. We were now fully loaded and began the journey home via Colombo and Aden, then through the Suez Canal into the Mediterranean. The weather was scorching as we steamed through the Red Sea, heading to Aden for more supplies. Later, we anchored in the bitter lakes, giving most of us time for a swim in the cool waters.

The last time I had been in Aden I had managed to get heat exhaustion and I did not want to repeat that experience ever again. We were on the last part of our journey home as we cleared Port Said into the Mediterranean, our first port of call being Tilbury in Essex. We passed the rock of Gibraltar in thick fog, not actually managing to see the rock on this journey, having to reduce our speed until the fog cleared. We steamed northwards then eastwards down the English Channel until the pilot began guiding us into Tilbury harbour.

Time had flown as it was now the beginning of July 1955 and very shortly I would be going on leave. It was time to pack and start thinking about trains instead of ships. It was then time for the goodbyes, Captain Westlake first, then the Chief Officer, the sparks (radio officer) and the rest of the officers. I telephoned for my taxi, which came speeding down the quay and took me to the local station. I caught my train from King's Cross Station and was home in no time, catching a bus to my village. Mother and Pamela were waiting for me as I had despatched a telegram from Tilbury telling them of my arrival.

Greetings and kisses seem to last a long time. However, I still had the stories of my voyage to tell and neither my mother nor Pamela seemed to tire of them when they were repeated over and over again to friends and neighbours.

It was now July and some of my friends suggested that I go and work with them on the local farms as it was now haystacking time. It was a pleasant time spent with my friends. I used muscles that I didn't even know I had, and the dust caused me to sneeze all the time. We had to use pitchforks to toss the straw onto the tractor's trailer before another empty trailer would appear before us. I was actually quite pleased this time when a letter arrived telling me when my leave was to end and what ship I would be joining.

I was told to report to Liverpool to rejoin my previous ship, the *City of New York*, again as acting Fourth Officer. It was now 2 August and the ship quickly moved into dry dock to have the hull scrubbed and painted. As there was no cargo work going on at that time, we were allowed to go ashore most evenings. One evening I went along with some of my work mates into the centre of Liverpool. I was being taken to a local dance hall called 'Reeces'. I had the most wonderful evening and although not a good dancer, I managed to dance all night long. It was on that evening that I met my future wife, Patricia. We both enjoyed ourselves tremendously, Patricia showing me all the dance moves and me having to apologise several times for stepping on her toes. I made a date to take her to the pictures to see a film that she had been longing to see. I was overjoyed to have my first girlfriend, someone who was willing to write to me while I was away at sea.

A fortnight later the ship moved out of dry dock to Birkenhead to load over seven thousand tons of cargo. My thoughts were elsewhere now that I had a girlfriend, but with the ship only being docked in Birkenhead, I managed to see her at least twice a week.

When you are enjoying life, you want it to go on forever, but unfortunately that is not always the case. The next day I had to ring Patricia to tell her that I would be departing for India the following Sunday. That Saturday night was extra special but as the ship was leaving at 6 a.m. I could not stay out too late.

Once again, we were steaming down the Mediterranean for Port Said, eventually arriving in Bombay where we dropped anchor and began unloading the cargo into barges. We had to use our own winches to move heavy lift cranes and locomotive train engines, which often weigh up to fifty tons. We then had cargo for Pakistan to unload so we headed off to Karachi, but we got message to make all speed for Cochin in south-west India. The Chief Officer, Mr Pryde, was diagnosed by our doctor as having suffered a heart attack and he had to leave the ship immediately. We then steamed a few miles south to Alleppey where we had to anchor, again using our own winches to load four hundred tons of mats and bales of coir, and then head back to Cochin to load tea. We then went to Calicut on the Manganese coast of India to load ilmanite sand. It was now time to leave India on a homeward-bound journey, travelling through the Indian Ocean and stopping in Port Said to refuel.

We arrived in Liverpool on 17 November with all my

thoughts being of Patricia. The Captain had recommended that I take my Second Officer's Certificate as I had had sufficient sea time, so I proposed to enrol at the Liverpool College of Technology on the navigation course. Mind you, having a girlfriend in Liverpool was the deciding factor! I enrolled at the college before embarking on the train journey home. My mother was delighted that I had decided to enrol at college, for I was following in my father's footsteps, and she was willing me to succeed.

I eventually packed my things but this time I would be staying in a new town and not heading straight back to join another ship. I caught the train to Liverpool and as recommended sought accommodation in the officers' club in Canning Street. I commuted daily to the Liverpool College of Commerce, where I met pupils and lecturers. The course was hard, but I had my girlfriend to help boost my confidence. Patricia was my anchor, and when I did not feel like working, she encouraged me and I eventually managed to pass both my written and verbal examinations. This was followed by a big celebration with Patricia's brothers, a few pints of beer were supped that day and I received a telegram from my mother expressing her joy, which made my day.

It was time to pack my things and all the books and papers that I had accumulated over the weeks and headed home to see my mother. I planned to see Patricia before I left and wanted to ask her to marry me. Patricia was sorry that I was leaving Liverpool but when I broached the subject of getting engaged it brought a magnificent smile to her face. It was painful parting and I almost missed the bus as I couldn't stop kissing and holding her. We had one last kiss before I rushed up the avenue to catch my bus.

I took a taxi the next day to Liverpool Lime Street giving the cab driver a generous tip as he helped me with my load of baggage. The train went via Manchester and Sheffield before eventually rolling into my station. I had to get a taxi from the railway station to the bus station where I waited an hour for my bus. Having so many parcels with me, the bus conductor had to help me onto the bus, which was crowded as it was market day. I finally reached home where crowds of villagers were there to greet me and I guessed that my mother must have told them about my recent success.

My mother rushed up to me and gave me an affectionate kiss on my cheek. My sister too was waiting to give me a hug. She was sitting in her new wheelchair, which I knew she would want me to mention, which, of course, I did. My mother wanted all the details, so we waved goodbye to the crowd of villagers and went inside. She asked her questions and we talked a great deal, before she handed me a letter which I knew would be from my girlfriend. I had to explain all about my new love and asked my mother if it would be possible to have Patricia come for a visit.

The next day I replied to Patricia suggesting that we meet halfway as she had not travelled so far before. Within a couple of days her reply came accepting my proposition and a date and time were made. We met at Sheffield Station and made the last part of the journey together. I could see that Patricia had made a special effort with her appearance for the family meeting. Everything worked out perfectly, with all parties enjoying each other's company, the time passing quickly as never before. I travelled halfway to Liverpool with my girlfriend, despite protests that she would be fine.

The letter from my company arrived a few days later

instructing me to join my old ship, the *City of New York*, in New York as Third Officer. This meant that I would have to travel out to America, flying from Heathrow Airport. I had never flown on a cruiser across the Atlantic before. I had to write to my girlfriend telling her about my arrangements, therefore delaying our engagement for a while longer. I hoped that Patricia would wait for me.

The hotel in London was booked where I was to stay for one night before getting a taxi to the airport. The flight was smooth and it amazed me that passengers were walking up and down the plane and I found out later that they had been going to the bar. I was soon to follow, having a few cold beers and chatting to several people at the bar. That day I had two breakfasts, one on the plane and the second aboard the *City of New York*.

CHAPTER XI

City of New York: The Third Trip

I was met at the airport by the company's agent and driven by him directly to Brooklyn and the ship. Nothing much had changed in the three months I had been away. A few of the crew were new to me, but not the Captain. The Chief Officer Mr Bradley called me up to his cabin. He said, 'The skipper is a bit of a stickler for discipline young man so be very careful.' I just said, 'Yes sir,' but did not tell him that I had sailed with the Captain before.

I knocked on the Captain's door and he shouted 'Come in,' and with a hand thrust out he said, 'Right young man, I told you that if you worked hard I had every confidence in you to succeed, right now we have met again. You carry on and do your level best with everything and we will get on like a house on fire.' I knew that some of his officers thought that he ran his ships like the Navy, everything done to time, but you knew where you stood with him and I liked him. I think it was because I could imagine my father being in the same mould as Captain Westlake.

Our voyage to India began in earnest next day. We steamed off down the Hudson River and across the Atlantic at a full speed of sixteen knots. We were soon passing Gibraltar and into the Mediterranean. As usual, we had to stop temporarily in Aden to take on board fuel oil and water, then we steamed on to Karachi before going on to Bombay. We saw many

Doha's sailing back home with their white sails painting a picturesque sight as the sun was setting and gleaming off them. India has a distinct smell and floating by us on the breeze were the myriad smells of curry and cooking fish. As we slowed our engines to enter Bombay harbour, flying fish often landed on our decks, floundering and gasping for seawater and oxygen.

We had almost all our cargo to unload. The Indian stevedores were waiting to board the ship as we moored into the dock, ready to start work. I had been writing to Patricia my usual love letters. However, I hoped that I had written them well and that she would appreciate them.

Most of my colleagues were waiting patiently for our shipping agent to appear with our letters from home. You could tell by their expressions if a nice letter had been received. A sour face could mean no letter or, worse, a letter with bad news, like a girlfriend going off with someone else. That day I had received a lovely letter, which my face obviously betrayed as my friends sang out 'She loves you, yeah, yeah, yeah.' I had to laugh, but inside I could feel my heart pounding. I tore open the envelope from my girlfriend and read it, trying to savour the words, but my love was too strong. I ducked behind a ventilator funnel and reread the letter from start to finish.

The sound of the steel cargo hook hitting the side of the steel hatch brought me back to reality and to my job of supervising the discharge of the cargo. Fortunately, I was dressed in my working clothes, so when the Chief Officer popped his head round the corner to check we were all working, I looked the part. The routine of going up and down the hatches commenced once again. The Bombay dockers worked hard and very long hours, so the discharge of our British cargo was soon finished. We left the quay at the end of the week proceeding south to Cochin. We had to ensure that the tea chests were stored correctly so that they would not move about if we encountered rough weather. I found out that we would then go on to Madras on the east coast next.

We arrived in Madras three days later with a message to go straight into the harbour. Our pilot helped us guide the ship into the harbour to begin loading the cargo. I knew that night that I should endeavour to complete my letter to Patricia so that it could be posted off home. I learnt that we were to anchor in the harbour, which meant moving off from the dock and then loading from barges. This is slower and can add days onto your voyage. I noticed that the bales had a destination of New York written on the side of them, so it appeared that after leaving India we would be heading across the Atlantic. Bradley, the Chief Officer, was standing beside me and it was as though he had read my mind. 'Peter, our next port of call will not be New York but Calcutta. Well, it better had be, as that is where I am to be relieved of duty. Then you will be heading to New York.' This was a rule that I was beginning to learn increasingly – that is, assume nothing.

The next day we steamed out of Madras heading north, it being day's run to Calcutta. We steamed up the Hougli River where the water was calm, although the river ran quite quickly and was wide in parts. We passed small villages on the edge of the water and could see smoke curling up skywards from the fires the inhabitants had built. The Indians were throwing their nets into the river hoping to catch their meal for the day, and waving at us as we passed.

We had to anchor just off the dock entrance to wait for any

spaces to become available in the harbour. We waited for two days. Those who were being relieved in Calcutta were lucky, as a launch had brought out their replacements, Mr Fairhurst our new Chief Officer and Mr Lambe, the new Second Officer. The launch also brought a smile to the rest of us on board as it had brought our eagerly awaited letters with it.

It was these letters from wives and girlfriends that kept us sane. I was so much in love at this time that I do not know how I would have reacted if I had not received a letter from my darling Patricia. This was not the case though and a beautiful letter was sent that made my day. I asked the Chief Officer if I could go to my cabin to read it. As he was new aboard the ship, he enquired about my duties and once he knew that I was on anchor watch until we moved into the harbour, he allowed me fifteen minutes alone. I avidly read the letter before charging upstairs to report again for anchor watch. The following day another launch was sent, this time carrying our pilot, so we were soon steaming into our berth in the Calcutta dock.

The dockers were soon aboard the ship and when the last rope was tied to the quay bollard, the gangway was lowered. The harbour cranes were soon swinging into action and they started to discharge the cargo from the holds. We were expecting to be in Calcutta for a week or so as we not only had to discharge our cargo, but also had to load the Indian raw materials to take elsewhere.

A few friends and I were decidedly fed up with the mundane routine and thought it would be a good idea to have an evening ashore. We started off by having a few quiet drinks in the Grand Hotel Gardens. That evening the hotel had a six-piece band playing and we stayed there for a couple of hours before Dave suggested that we try somewhere else. We all decided that we were feeling rather hungry so we headed for the Mogambo restaurant. We had a delicious meal of chicken mayonnaise with a fruit salad to follow. We had liked the Grand Hotel Gardens, so we decided to give it another try. As we arrived, we noticed that the floorshow was about to begin with a French vocalist and a line up of French can-can girls. There was a dance floor but the European girls looked so aloof that non of us even attempted to ask any of them to dance. In any case, most of the women were escorted.

The drink, food and setting were perfect, but alas we had no ladies to share the evening with. We all just chatted and enjoyed the rest of the evening, however. It was great to be away from the ship but, unfortunately, the time passed too quickly and the evening was coming to an end as it was 1.30 a.m. We all staggered aboard the ship shouting goodbyes to one another. We had to make straight for our bunks as wake-up at 6.30 a.m. soon comes around.

The completion of the discharge of our cargo and the loading of the cargo for America was soon finished and the next day we went down the Hougli River to Sri Lanka and then up the north Indian coast to Cochin on the Malabar coast.

Two or three days later we picked up our pilot to guide us into Cochin harbour, as usual dropping anchor. We had two thousand tons of cargo to load from barges with our ship's derricks and noisy steam winches. We completed the loading pretty quickly as the dockers worked through the night. The Junior Officers were all extremely tired, often having very little sleep. The ship with the guidance pilot aboard steamed out of Cochin, all whistles making a terrific noise and encouraging the seagulls overhead to shriek wildly. The sea was calm for the moment as we set course for Aden to take on fresh supplies.

We steamed through the Mediterranean after going through the Indian Ocean and passed through the Suez Canal without incident. To find our position each day the Captain would have all the Navigation Officers on the bridge with their sextants taking sights of the sun. We each had our own log and navigation tables and it became a race to work out our position, each of us flicking through the tables and making the calculating. We took sights in the morning using the chronometer to calculate our longitude and worked out our latitude at noon. It is much easier today with satellite navigation and possibly more accurate. We headed past the heights of Gibraltar and into the North Atlantic, where the swell was running viciously. The ship pitched and rolled so that sea spray covered our bows and the foredeck. There was little to see as we headed further into the Atlantic, but we had to remain alert and keep our eyes on the horizon. We took turns in foggy weather to watch the radar screen.

Boston was our first port of call, most of us having visited the city before, so there were few surprises. We stopped briefly to take on our pilot who would help guide us into the dock and harbour. We were soon discharging the cargo from India.

It was quite cold as it was now the middle of October. We were dressed in our blue uniform so we were equipped for this kind of weather; our tropical kit now safely packed away in our cabins. I was due to be relieved in New York, having been on the ship for six months, and I was looking forward to going home. However, disappointment was to follow when the Captain called me up to his cabin. He told me that he had received new orders and that I was due to be relieved the next time that the ship would be in America, that would be in another six months! The disappointment enveloped me and the thought of not seeing my girlfriend for another six months was unbearable.

With the Gulf crisis came a message from our agent. We were told to go to the South African coast then to the Cape of Good Hope before heading out to Pakistan and India. The Suez Canal was a short cut to Pakistan and India from Europe and, as one of the officers pointed out to me, rounding the Cape of Good Hope meant that the voyage was almost turning out to be a world cruise! The sights of the South African coast were new to me and I at least had one thing to look forward to.

We steamed out of New York harbour and down the Hudson River again with the pilot pacing about on the bridge. We steamed across the Atlantic, moving more south-east now, as our first port of call would now be Mombassa on the east coast of Africa. To get there we had to steam round the Cape of Good Hope where we could see white houses lining the shore.

The sun shone out onto an almost clear blue sky, dazzling me as it reflected brightly off the sea. We passed Cape Town, but as we were ten miles off the coast, it was difficult to see anything. Our two South African apprentices asked if they could come up on the bridge. I beckoned them to come and allowed them a quick ten minutes. They were naturally very disappointed that we were not stopping in Cape Town because being relieved in Mombassa meant a long journey home. We got a very brief look at Table Mountain before steaming eastwards, passing Durban and then going up the Mozambique Channel, where we picked up our pilot to guide us into Mombassa harbour. I did not know then that this port would become so familiar to me.

We had to anchor, as all the berths were full, and wait for a ship to sail or steam out, so that we could take its position. Les brought up our letters shortly after. 'Sorry Pete, only one for you,' and then seeing my face, his hand went behind his back and produced another four letters for me, two from mother and two from Patricia. I was too happy to shout at Les for his quite distressing joke! I just wanted to read the letters, particularly the one from my girlfriend.

Mother gave me the news that she and Pamela were moving with her friend Tom to Lincolnshire. Tom was a blacksmith and had bought the blacksmith's shop in the village of Upton, about five miles from the town of Gainsborough. I quickly read the letter from Patricia to see if she still loved me. I was becoming more lovesick; absence was truly making my heart grow fonder every day.

We steamed off after taking on board our guidance pilot to take us out of the harbour. We had only been in port two days but despite that, we loaded fuel oil and fresh water and more stores. Our new destination was Karachi; the weather was now warming up even more.

When the ship was docked one evening, the talk was about our athletes and their performance. Much criticism was bandied about, which I objected to and I suggested that rather than criticising, the only way to resolve the argument was to see who could win the mile race. Before I knew it, my silly jest had turned into a full race, with the Chief Officer suddenly becoming my manager, charging anyone an entrance fee of one rupee. He suggested that anyone who beat me would result in me buying that person six pints of beer. Running in that heat was really silly. However, I could not see a way of backing out of the race gracefully. I might have been a good runner at school, but that was a few years previous. I had ten men against me but what was at stake were the drinks I had to buy and my pride.

The next day, the news had spread around the ship and I found a crowd of people of every description shouting and cheering. We, the competitors, were also an assorted bunch dressed in different shirts and shorts. We started the race on the Chief Officer's whistle. The course had been measured out on one of the ship charts. I found the race exhausting but with my pride at stake, I was pretty determined. Some of the crew had found bicycles to ride on. I think that if a film crew had been present it may well have been a classic comedy clip. Fortunately, a six-foot tall engineer was the only one to beat me, and as we staggered across the chalk line we shook hands together, both vowing never to do that again. From that moment, I was nicknamed 'Chris Chattaway'. I was pleased as the race had been a success and it had not cost me much money and those overweight had lost a bit from sweating in the heat! For weeks afterwards the conversation was centred on the race. A return match was suggested, but fortunately, it did not materialise for lack of enthusiasm.

Karachi, I was pleased to see, was being left behind in our wake, and three days later as we steamed south for Bombay. We had over three thousand tons of cargo and our Indian cargo of jute and other raw materials to load, so we would be there more than a week. It looked like we would be spending Christmas Day in the city.

I had been told that the engineer who beat me in the race was a really good runner and had expected to win, so I didn't feel so bad at being beaten by him and at not winning the race. Our next sporting activity turned out to be a game of football. A Swedish ship's crew had challenged us to play against their team in Bombay. It turned out to be a very hard match for us. I was chosen to play centre forward, although my normal position was in defence. I found out early on that I was the target for their toughest players and although we did not win, I did manage to score two goals.

I became very bruised with the tough treatment I received. The Swedes were not prepared to lose and their shirts bore their ship's crest and their team was much better prepared than ours was. I had to have treatment from our doctor for all my cuts and bruises. My injuries prevented me seeing more of the city but my friends did persuade me to share their taxis to see the film Rock Around the clock.

The cinema was six miles away, so I could see why they wanted me to share their taxi and help pay the fare! We all enjoyed the film, but being on the outskirts of the city it was quite a journey. One of my friends, Les, was having trouble with his throat and our doctor advised him to go to the local hospital. The doctors at the hospital, after examining his throat, said that his tonsils were too inflamed to be operated on immediately and explained that they could not operate until the swelling had eased. I went to the hospital to visit him and joked that I had just seen one of his doctors sharpening the hospital carving knife. A doctor had told him that it would be Boxing Day before they could remove his tonsils. The hospital overlooked Beach Kandy Swimming Pool, so trying to cheer him up I said, 'Les you have a wonderful view from your ward window.' He replied by saying, 'Pete, ensure that the ship does not sail without me, won't you?' I just said yes, but perhaps he realised that there was little that I could do.

We steamed out of Bombay on Boxing Day, heading for Madras with a short stop in Colombo for more fuel oil and fresh water. We were in Madras just in time to discharge some more of the cargo, then steamed north to the Hourly River and further up the river to Calcutta. The sun was lovely even in January, unlike my home town where they were possibly suffering the worst month of the English winter. The last letter I had received made me shiver, but it was only Patricia's description about the cold weather she had to endure! Otherwise, her letters left me feeling very hot, yearning to hold her in my arms and kiss her sweet lips.

As we steamed south, from the bridge I could see far away the coastline of Sri Lanka. It looked exceedingly attractive with the light green coconut palms contrasting with the dark brown mountains. We passed about a hundred fishing boats. They were, or appeared, so small like canoes, but the whole population of the villages appeared to be out fishing. The ship came closer to the boats and I was pleased that I could not understand the language as the natives shouted and pointed at us as our bow wave rocked their boats. The fishing boats were tossed about like corks, but I could do nothing to help them. Maybe next time they saw a ship the size of ours they would keep well away.

We expected to be in Colombo harbour for only two or three days for we had only some more tea cargo to load for the USA and oil fuel and water for our own use. Writing to Patricia, we were both thinking on paper about the wedding plans and changing companies to find one that only did a maximum of three months away from Britain. It was a frustrating feeling for I did not want to leave the Ellerman Hall Line. Where I had been enjoying my voyages and making new friends, I was at that time and remained that way for years very much in love with Patricia and being absent from her was becoming very hard.

The voyage continued with us steaming into Colombo harbour and picking up our guidance pilot who showed us where to anchor in the bay. We, the officers, were on anchor watch and on cargo duties and we stayed there for two days until the cargo was loaded, and fuel oil and fresh water and stores taken on board.

We then steamed off around Sri Lanka, South Africa and into the Atlantic, steaming through the mounting seas and the heavy swell towards America with small patches of fog, where the radar was needed. On ship we had with us apprentices and a Fourth Officer, two people on duty on each watch on the bridge when it was foggy, one person on each watch being the minimum on radar watch. The radar screen showed up any obstruction and even icebergs would show up if looked for alertly. It did need practice to work the radar but the fog soon cleared and all of us were almost cheering. We were now close to the American coast, the first port of call being Boston where we stayed for two days discharging our Indian cargo.

Some of us old hands – including me, of course – were hoping that at our next port we would be relieved to allow us to go home to our loved ones. The next port of call was

Baltimore. Therefore, our pilot had to guide us up the Chesapeake River to the entrance of Baltimore harbour. The docks fortunately were not crowded and we were allowed to dock straight away, which brought smiles to our faces.

Our next task was to await the arrival of our reliefs. It was an extremely cold morning standing on the deck. First came the company agent with our letters from home. He was surrounded by bodies like a rugby scrum, as the crew all wanted their letters first, so I stood back. I was also anxious to get news of when I was going home on the *Queen Elizabeth*, the Cunard liner, which happened about two weeks later from New York.

I was on duty on the navigation bridge when the guidance pilot and Captain were each shouting orders at me. It was night-time and we narrowly escaped a collision with a large oil tanker. There had been two collisions in New York harbour where several people had been killed in thick fog. I expect that it was natural that people on our ship were on edge. We dropped anchor in the river, which saved us from hitting or colliding with the tanker. Everyone on the bridge was breathing heavily and I did not want to be in that situation again. Almost all of us were also shaking.

Our thoughts soon returned, or at least mine did to getting home and seeing my lovely Patricia. I had, as with most of the others, begun furiously writing letters home to post them when the ship docked, but not knowing anything definite was not easy. I wanted to get engaged to Patricia on my next leave home, or at least soon, and when we both were off work together so that we would have time to go out and buy the engagement ring.

With our guidance pilot on board we steamed into Baltimore harbour. It reminded me of the last time I had been there when I had had my appendix removed. This time I was only thinking about the relief Third Officer to appear so that I could plan my visit home. I needed first to pack all of my things so that nothing was forgotten.

CHAPTER XII

Going Home

Once back in my cabin and having started to pack, I was amazed at the amount of stuff that I had collected in the ten months I had been on ship. There was a knock on my cabin door. My relief had arrived and it was perfect timing seeing as my clothes and other items were packed in my suitcase. The drawers of my cabin were clean and empty ready for the new officer and his things. I showed him round the ship after having a quick chat and shaking his hand. Two of us were leaving the *City of New York*, Les and I, and we were both travelling by train to New York to catch the Cunard liner from there to Liverpool. I was delighted that we were travelling together. I even tried to send a radio telegram home with the news, but was out of luck on that count.

Our train journey to New York went quickly, perhaps because Les and I got on so well together. Once in the city, we took a yellow taxi cab down to the Liner Pier and were soon aboard the liner, sharing adjacent cabins. It was a familiar scene, almost like a busman's holiday, for Les and I, and we settled in quickly by putting away our things. Next, we heard the steward saying it was the last call for dinner. Les and I hurriedly washed and shaved and dashed for our meal, which was beautifully served.

The chatter and laughter echoed round the large dining saloon which was pleasant but which we had not been used to before. A stout gentleman with plenty of gold braid stood up and banged his gavel. 'All please stand for the grace,' he said. We stood until he said 'Sit ladies and gentleman, enjoy your food.' We did just that, and then a waiter with a silver plate served food onto our plates.

When we were halfway across the Atlantic, the loud-speakers crackled and the Commodore announced that Cunard was sorry to announce to passengers were not going direct to England as per the schedule because of a small trade dispute. The ship was going to dock at Cherbourg in France and from there we would be transferred to another liner to take us to Liverpool. A mass of groans from almost all passengers went round the ship. Les and I were more philosophical than most, however. We quietly wondered what the labour dispute was all about. We found out later it was caused by a passenger removing their own baggage, which the baggage staff said was part of their job and they blacked that particular liner. We docked in Cherbourg two days later. A small Cunard ship moored alongside and the baggage was transferred for those passengers operating from Liverpool.

As we were Merchant Navy personnel, Les and I received special treatment once the smaller Cunard liner moored in Liverpool. We shared a taxi from the ship to the centre of Liverpool. I had to see Patricia before going home to see my mother and sister. I thus had to change taxis to get my own taxi to Anfield. The moment I had been waiting for had at last arrived, and with many hugs and kisses I dropped onto one knee and proposed to Patricia. She agreed. We then discussed about buying a ring, it being unbeknown to Patricia that I had already seen a ring that she had liked. She was extremely happy as I was. I had already told her in my letter that money would not be a problem for the ring. She also liked an eternity ring, which matched the engagement ring, for which I agreed to buy and for which I got the most wonderful kiss. It is a special moment that I will treasure forever for we were both lovesick. I said, 'Patricia. Now darling, you can make those wonderful wedding plans but don't forget the date will have to be when I can find out when I am going to be on leave.'

My Patricia – at least I could write that now as she would soon be my wife. We had discussed by letter that I change shipping companies to one that did not do voyages longer than three or four months, because, being very lovesick, I could not stand being away from Patricia for very long. Ellerman Hall Line was a wonderful shipping company where I had made many friends. However, my love for Patricia was overpowering everything else.

It was lovely that Patricia, now my fiancée, had been down to Lincolnshire and had met my mother and sister. They had got on well and approved of our plans to get married. It was another hurdle overcome because now all I had to think about was joining my new shipping company. I had spoken to many people on my last ship, the *City of New York*, which shipping company they recommended, but as usual, opinions were divided. I had done my own research and decided that being in Liverpool my choice would have to be made quickly whilst still in that city. I was fortunate to be given an interview early the next morning. The interview resulted in my joining Palm Line Shipping Company sailing out of Liverpool to West Africa. I was told that a letter would be sent to my home address with the details of my joining instructions on my first Palm Line ship.

During the interview I had explained that I need first a month's leave at home in Lincolnshire, which was agreed. After saying goodbyes to my fiancée, I set off to Liverpool Lime Street Station for the journey to Lincolnshire. I found by the directions I was given that my train left from Liverpool Central Station in thirty minutes. With my case and other items, I quietly walked down the road to the station, caught my train and in three hours or more was hugging my mother and sister.

My leave went quickly. On a dry spring day, my friends and I went for a walk in the country. The farmers were working in the fields with tractors, getting the fields prepared for the planting of crops. My letter arrived that morning with my joining application. I was to join the Kumasi Palm in Tilbury, Essex. Therefore, I had to find out how to get there by train and what the train times were. However, I was by now quite used to doing it and had a list of train enquiry numbers and a small timetable.

Arriving in Tilbury – fortunately I got a train to the docks this time – the ship had only just arrived. Because it was still early on Sunday, the docks were deserted almost as if a nuclear alert had been called. I found that I was almost the first up the gangway. I was the relief Third Officer. The other Third Officer was waiting for me and was anxious to hand over quickly as he had a train to Grimsby to catch where he lived. I did not feel like cargo supervision as I had little sleep on the way down to the port.

CHAPTER XIII

Kumasi Palm and the Mendi Palm

Examining my cabin, I was surprised at how small it was. However, it did not take me long to put away my things. Although the *Kumasi Palm* was quite old, I did not expect to be on board for more than few weeks as I was only a relief officer and the original Third Officer had already left for his leave.

Even for a short time, getting up early each day to be ready for the dock workers to come on board at 8 a.m. to ensure the cargo was loaded properly was a tiring business. For a change being off duty, I walked into the next small town of Grays, and stood along with the crowd watching the multicoloured parade and procession with dancers and banners streaming and waving. The sun that day was streaming down, unlike the previous day, which had been wet and windy. That day had been a pleasant change for me seeing so much fun and laughter with the children really enjoying the clowns with their coloured cloaks and pointed hats. I almost skipped and ran back to the ship.

Next day, or the day after, brought some good news, the Third Officer my relief was returning and I was given ten days leave. The news was that after my leave I was to join another ship, the *Mendi Palm* also in Tilbury. It might even be in the next dock. However, because I intended to go to Liverpool to see my fiancée and also travel to Lincolnshire to see my mother and my sister, it meant a lot of travelling. It turned out not to be a lot of travelling, however.

First, I went home to my mother and sister in Lincolnshire to pick up some things I had left there and I left there some items that I did not need on the next voyage. Patricia, my fiancée, had asked me to go with her to her friend Margaret's wedding on the 1 June. It was not easy to plan so far ahead in the Merchant Navy because one did not know where one would be at a particular time.

Therefore, Patricia had written to me months or weeks earlier. I could not tell her then if I could go with her, but now I could say that I could. We wrote long love letters to each other, but letters – however lovely – were no substitute to being close, being able to kiss and the intimate events that take place between most lovers. Now I could really think that we would only be apart for a matter of days not weeks. My wish was to hold her close to me.

When I had joined the Merchant Navy, I had imagined that it would be a jolly good adventure and not something that would happen to me. I was now seriously in love with Patricia, wanting to kiss her lovely lips and hold her close. The dreams that you read about were actually happening to me! I am sure that being apart makes the love grow stronger, as it did for both of us that year. We were determined that our love would last a long, long time. If we had any problems, we would try to sit down and discuss the best way around the situation.

Now on board the *Mendi Palm*, the few days at home had flown by and even more so in Liverpool with Patricia. We had gone together to my friends wedding and I remember especially the wedding reception, the lovely food and the atmosphere. I nudged Patricia gently and said the next time we would be at a reception like this it will be our own wedding reception and she would be the centre of attraction. She said, 'In that case I shall be even be more nervous with everyone looking my way.'

We had arranged where we could go on honeymoon and had booked the hotels. This time the ship had to be on time as no delays were allowed. Our only problem turned out to be a matter of religion. My fiancée was a Catholic and I was Church of England, but Patricia had given way and had booked our wedding in the local Church of England church near her home. It was fantastic of her to do that. My mother had discussed all the issues with her at first hand, face to face, and they had got on very well together. Mother had said to Patricia that she did not mind where we got married, as long as we were happy and she had realised how much in love we were and that nothing else mattered.

We had some good news for us Junior Officers as we would have a break from climbing up and down hold ladders for a week whilst the ship went into dry dock to get the hull scraped, and some small repairs done. Rumours as usual were going around the ship what the departure date would be once the repairs were completed, and that it should be by the end of the week. It was now July and the weather had been so warm that I, including those not working, could lie in the sun wearing only a pair of shorts so that we got a bit of a tan.

At sea at last, we steamed out of Tilbury and down the Thames, dropping our pilot at the bar lightship in the river estuary. We were heading through the Bay of Biscay to the Canary Islands to refuel in Las Palmas and to take on more stores and fresh water. Our Second Officer, Lance, my senior, was a happy and friendly fellow and he was an easy man to work alongside. He lived in my fiancée's city of Liverpool, and he told me when we got chatting that he had been married for five years and lived in his wife's parents house until they had saved enough money to buy their own. It struck me how similar my own life may be in the future.

At sea, work is not difficult for Navigating Officers. My watch duty on the navigating bridge was from eight at night until twelve and the same hours in the morning, with my relief, Lance, coming on duty at twelve noon and at midnight. We also worked together, relieving one another for breakfast and lunch, which gave us the chance to talk, if nothing else took preference. The days passed quite quickly. We were now close to the Canary Islands and our guidance pilot to take us into Las Palmas harbour would soon be on board.

I now had a problem, because whilst I wanted to get home quickly to see my darling Pat, if I did so my money would be insufficient to last. Ideally, if we arrived home by the beginning of October, it would be better from the financial point of view as well as for our wedding arrangements. Therefore, I watched the calendar carefully.

We now had left the Canary Islands behind, as well as the grey skies and rough sea, heading as we were for Freetown in Sierra Leone. Whilst in port the company had kindly put on board a table tennis table, so that those not on duty or those with less urgent tasks to complete could play table tennis. In the early stages, several of us lost the light plastic balls into the sea due to wild shots, and we soon learnt that such shots should not be attempted! The sea was fairly calm and the sun beat down so that those playing table tennis had the sweat running off them in streams. The sweat made our hands very slippery and we found it difficult to keep a tight grip on our bats. If the weather changed and the swell got up, it would be even more difficult to play for keeping one's balance would be tricky if the ship began to roll heavily.

Lance informed me that it was the rainy season in West Africa and shortly after speaking to him the rain poured down, pattering loudly on the steel deck plates. The table tennis tables had to be hurriedly moved away and sun bathing was over for that day. The cargo of cement would be quick to discharge but would create a fine mist of dust everywhere. Lance had suggested that we would only be in Freetown for two days at most. Sure enough, he was correct again, and in less than two days we were steaming down the West African coast to the port of Takoradi in Nigeria.

It was very hot in the afternoon between the rain showers. In fact, within minutes one could fry an egg on the deck plates! We arrived of Takoradi in the early hours and had to wait until daybreak before the pilot would guide us into the harbour because he said that entrance was a bit difficult and he needed full daylight to see everything.

There was no rest for us Navigation Officers, however, for once into harbour we were off the ship's navigation bridge and, after a quick change into working clothes, supervising the discharge of the cargo from the holds. The cement dust spread even further than I had imagined, because the paper sacks split very easily. By nightfall I was very tired, having only had four hours' sleep the night before, and climbing up and down our hold ladders all day long. The African dockers worked long hours, which, of course, meant that we had to supervise the discharge and loading of cargo for them. I was starting at 6 a.m. and finishing at 9 p.m., and had almost run out of paper calculating when we would arrive home! Patricia – naturally – was waiting for me to give her a definite date so that she could book our wedding in the church. She had volunteered also to book the car, flowers and the reception. If the date was not correct, it would disappoint many people and cost us much money in deposits and other associated costs.

It was now near the end of September. I had estimated that we would dock on the 14 October and, in fact, we docked in Glasgow – our home port – on 10 October 1957. I cannot take the credit for my estimate, however, for I had a great deal of help from Lance who had more experience than I and who had done the same calculations for his own wedding five years before. Lance gave me many more tips, thinking of his own wedding and approved of our choice of destination for the honeymoon.

I had been round several places on the West African coast, the Creek ports of Warri and Burutu, where the jungle goes down to the river edge, and to Accra where we had to anchor as close in the shore as possible as the cargo had to be lowered by our winches on to beach boats lashed together. The Africans paddling the beach boats always went to the nearest ship. There were huge logs weighing up to several tons each with dockers using wires through metal hooks in the holds to manoeuvre the logs into position. Lance had told me to be more careful when the logs were being moved in position because one never knew when the wire would break and if one was in the way one could lose an arm or a leg. I was very careful and remembered his words for a long time.

Loading was almost completed, and as soon as it was, we were homeward bound, the ship bringing me closer to marrying my lovely Patricia. The voyage was incident free and after stopping briefly for fuel oil and fresh water, we steamed through the Bay of Biscay, which this time was kinder to us apart from a heavy swell, the weather being normal for that time of year. We were now in our heavier blues, the Captain having asked us to change out of our tropical whites. It also meant that there were no delays for which I was more pleased about than normal this time because of my forthcoming marriage.

We steamed up the Clyde River to the Glasgow docks with our guidance pilot on board and we were on time with no delays. It was 10 October 1957. The dull grey sky did not match my mood, however, for I was very happy. The seagulls were screeching overhead as if they too had seen our arrival. My clothes and everything I possessed were packed ready for my departure. Our Chief Officer had told me that I could leave the ship just as soon as the ship's gangway was in place and when my relief had arrived.

The ship was moored with ropes and wires around a bollard on the quay and the gangway was lowered smoothly. The customs men were the first up and aboard to search the ship for items not declared. In those days, however, drugs were not a problem, but cigarettes, tobacco and alcohol were often discovered as were cameras and pricey items of clothing where the duty had not been paid.

My relief officer arrived allowing me, after the hand over, to get a taxi to Glasgow Central Station. The farewell good wishes were still ringing in my ears as the taxi with my luggage sped away. I was going first to see my mum and sister in Lincolnshire before going to Liverpool to see my beloved Patricia.

CHAPTER XIV

Home to Prepare for the Wedding

Once on the train I checked that I had everything with me, because my mind was full of other things and I was normally forgetful. This time I had to make sure that I had not forgotten anything and I found that I had everything. I got on the wrong train, however! I grabbed all my luggage and parcels and shouted to a porter to help me. He came and got a nice tip into the bargain, which he deserved, as he secured me a seat on the correct train. I breathed a sigh of relief as the train puffed out of Glasgow Central Station heading south.

The train clanked its way down the line and, after two changes, arrived at Retford. I then had to pay for a taxi to my mother's house, three miles further east. Fortunately, I had enough money to pay the taxi driver. Greetings and hugs from mother and Pamela were lovelier and more vigorous than I could remember, but that was because my Patricia had recently paid a visit and had made a big hit with my family. I unpacked with my mother by my side, her telling me what needed washing. She told me to leave everything and that she would sort out my things later. All I had to do was tell her what I wanted to take with me. 'You get out the iron and press your trousers and clean your shoes and when you have done that you will have to pass my inspection,' she said. This continued for two days and, at last, she was reasonably satisfied. She said, 'Now you can get out and see your friends. You should have two or three days before going off to see your fiancée in Liverpool.' I departed saying goodbye to mother and Pamela. However, it was cold and damp, being late autumn, and my friends were at home, though if the weather had been nicer they would have been in the local farmers' fields. We chatted and chatted and they laughed about my forthcoming marriage. Most had girlfriends but none were at the serious stage, therefore marriage was not on the agenda.

That evening, walking home, I was relaxed and happy. I knew that everything had to be in place for my momentous visit to Liverpool. Patricia had arranged that I stay with her auntie who lived in the next avenue. This would leave her free to get ready for the wedding. We had still to go the jewellers in the centre of Liverpool to buy the important little band of gold – her wedding ring. We now knew what needed to be done, so the planning could begin.

Mother, off course, needed to be consulted, as she too had to decide where in Liverpool she was going to stay for the wedding. She decided that she would write immediately to Mabel, her sister-in-law, to ask if she could stay with her. Mother reminded me to write to my best man, Jim, to ensure that he would arrive in Liverpool in good time for the wedding. I had asked him a few weeks previously and Jim had enthusiastically agreed and was getting time off ship especially for the wedding.

Patricia had planned to meet me off the train at Liverpool Central Station. Therefore, with mother almost pushing me and with everything packed and inspected by her, the taxi arrived and drove me to the local station with my luggage. With mother and Pamela waving and plenty of other people also waving and shouting, I had a sinking feeling that I had forgotten something. However, the feeling was soon replaced by feelings of excitement.

My lovely Patricia was there to meet me when the train at last pulled into Liverpool. After hugs and kisses, we decided to walk down Liverpool Church Street to a jewellers to buy the ring. Once in the jewellers, it didn't take very long before the assistant was rushing around the shop showing Patricia loads of wedding rings in trays. Patricia's choice was easy because she wanted a simple gold band.

After going into a coffee shop just a few doors away, when we returned the ring was ready for fitting. With a lovely smile – and kiss for me – we went back to the station for my luggage with the wedding ring safely tucked away in my upper jacket. Patricia was watching me carefully and reminding me constantly to make sure that it was kept safe.

We had no trouble getting a taxi home and it was there that I was staying until the day before our wedding. I was introduced soon after to Patricia's aunts. From there, I would be going with Patricia's brothers for my stag night.

CHAPTER XV

The Wedding to Patricia

As stag nights go, after warnings from many people, not least Patricia, it was a rather quiet affair: a few pints only and none 'spiked' either I was pleased to see and taste. Waking up in a strange house with the special day ahead of me had a way of sobering one up quickly. I felt on top of the world stepping into the car. A short journey up to the top of the avenue and we were outside the church with the photographer taking pictures and shouting instructions. I shook the hand of my best man, Jim.

We walked down the church aisle and from there I waved to my mother and her friend, Tom, and to all my relatives. The wedding was splendid and went by in a flash and in no time we were outside having the usual photographs taken and soon were whisked off to the reception. My lovely wife had booked the reception well and everyone enjoyed the day. Nothing went wrong, so we were both able to let out a big sigh of relief. We had planned to sneak away and go down to the station to start the honeymoon without anyone realising we had gone. However, somehow the word must have got to some of the guests, because Patricia – now my wife – was covered in confetti and even had some under her clothes for a day or two afterwards! Patricia even had to ask me to look for the confetti, which I removed carefully.

Our carriage window was scrawled with the words 'Just

Myself outside the Church of St Columba, Anfield, Liverpool, 1957.

Married' and we both just shook with laughter. We were both so happy and in love that nothing could spoil it. We arrived in London and got a taxi to our hotel. If we had known how close it was to the station, we could easily have walked, but there were small showers of rain. After a lovely dinner at the hotel, we decided to walk to Trafalgar Square. Dozens of other people also had the same idea. The pigeons were happy with the crowd of people and came down in their hundreds, expecting a big feast of bread and other seeds. We had both dressed for the rain and strolled around the square quite

Just married.

Patricia, now my wife, and me in Trafalgar Square, London, on our honeymoon, 1957.

happily. I reminded Patricia that we had a big day next day with the train journey to St Ives in Cornwall, so we walked slowly back to our hotel. The truth of the matter was that being a red-blooded male, I was eager to share my bed with my new wife.

An early morning call saw us awake for the new day. We had time only for a quick continental breakfast – i.e. no bacon, sausage or eggs – before we had to dash to our room to pack. We did not mind packing because we had hardly disturbed our cases. When the bill was paid the porter got us a taxi across London to Paddington Station. We had to search the station for our train, so I asked a porter. 'Not arrived yet sir, platform 12 it usually comes out on.' We walked to platform 12 and just as we arrived, a huge gush of steam enveloped us. When we could see again, The Cornish Express came into view – it was our train for the morning. We climbed aboard, I carrying our luggage, and found our seats in an almost empty carriage apart from a large middle-aged lady who almost immediately began humming a classical tune and fished in her bag for her knitting. I whispered to Patricia: 'A Margaret Rutherford look alike,' and she laughed. I did not think anyone would have possibly heard but the large lady said, 'Yes, they do say that I look like a Margaret Rutherford.' We smiled at her and Patricia, ever the diplomat, said, 'That is a lovely dress you are wearing, angora wool is it?' 'Yes,' she replied 'very observant of you dear.' The ice now broken, the conversation flowed with my wife, Patricia, and the Margaret Rutherford look alike.

The train journey to Cornwall took a long time. I had bought a small book at Paddington Station and reading it passed the time well. I looked up after a dig in the ribs from Patricia. We were passing along the Cornish coast. The scenery was marvellous; the purple-coloured heather on the moor and hillsides contrasted sharply with the white surf rolling in from the sea, the waves dashing onto the rocks.

The train at last came into St Ives Station. I was curious about the hotel we had chosen and also a little apprehensive. We had booked the Porthminster Hotel and the choice turned out to be superb one, for our room overlooked the beach and the sea beyond. When lying in bed in the morning with the curtains open we experienced the most wonderful view from the window. We could see a few hardy types, running across the beach with only their swimming trunks on. It was mild, but being October it gave me the shivers. I pointed them out to Patricia and she just laughed and said that it could not really be that cold and that it takes all kinds of people to make a world. At that point, I tickled her, and we snuggled down in the bed for another half an hour. That night, I took my wife to the small bar, and to celebrate our marriage I bought her a champagne cocktail. This was not the success I had intended.

The next day, when the sun shone and the cold wind had gone into hiding, we walked along the cliff path into St Ives Bay and saw the beautiful beaches, which must be lovely in the summer months, deciding to visit again in the summer one year. We wandered slowly around town and could easily see why it was thought of as an artist's paradise. The narrow streets and lovely shops displaying their wares were so quaint, and we found ourselves in an auction buying things which would not see the light of day, but we enjoyed ourselves.

We wandered down to the harbour and feeling brave and perhaps showing off a little – and having my towel and swimming trunks – I dived off the harbour wall and swam across the harbour. The water was cold, much colder than I had expected, and I was freezing when I got out. Patricia was laughing as she helped me dry. My wife had little sympathy for me and I vowed never to do that again.

We had both enjoyed being together on the honeymoon. It was about discovering one another as most of our courtship had been by letter. It was truly remarkable being able to reach out and touch one another. We both had similar tastes in many things such as music. We never really argued about anything; we were both so much in love with one another. Even the staff in the hotel commented on this fact to us both, separately. The days really sped by and soon the last day of the honeymoon was upon us. We talked about packing and started to collect our belongings and arrange the train and the taxi. Patricia said that when she had telephoned home she was told that there was a letter waiting for me.

Next morning, with all our luggage packed and our breakfast eaten, we got in the taxi, but not before paying the bill and thanking all the staff. The train north to Liverpool seemed faster than the train upon which we had arrived. We had a carriage almost to ourselves, which was very pleasant for we could hold hands in freedom. Patricia leaned over to me and said, 'do you know, Peter, we are almost an old married couple. It's almost two weeks since our wedding.' I nodded in agreement and said, 'But what if I have to leave you again soon after we get home to your house, or your father's house?' My wife pulled a face. 'Don't remind me about going to work. I can go back next week. You won't know when you are going until you open the envelope from Palm Line.' We just grabbed one another and kissed, not caring if it embarrassed the other passengers. 'Please call me Pat, not Patricia, my father and my brothers call me Pat.' I said, 'Darling, from now on to me you are Pat, not Patty, that you hate being.' She just laughed at that.

The journey home passed sweetly as we cuddled one another and held hands. We enjoyed each other's company very much. The train rolled into Lime Street Station, and with the luggage in a taxi the taxi driver shouted 'No confetti in my cab please!' We were perturbed; the driver pointed at one of our suitcases where the words 'JUST MARRIED' were written in white chalk. We thought how long had that notice been there? Then I remembered one of the young staff in the hotel with chalk on her hands and with a mischievous look on her face. I whispered the thought to Pat and she smiled.

Pat's father, George, opened the door almost before we knocked. Pat had fished a key from her handbag but it was not needed. Once we got inside the house George handed me three letters, the official letter from Palm Line being the first I opened. With my wife almost grabbing it, we read it together. I was to join the ship *Africa Palm* in Tilbury on Friday, 15 November, which was only in five days. Pat and I decided to saviour those five days. She reminded me that she had an interview for the big department store in Liverpool, G. H. Lee, on Tuesday, straight after lunch. I said, 'I would like to meet more people again but it would mean not missing the early morning bus into Liverpool. I am sure that your pleasant personality – if you don't worry – will come over well and you will get the job.'

The next day felt almost spring like, although it was late autumn. We decided to go to Chester, and having no car we went by bus, then walked down to the pier head from Liverpool Church Street and took the ferry to Birkenhead where we got the Chester bus. The town of Chester almost seemed 'old worlde' and very picturesque, with the River Dee very close to the town and shops. The sun shone brightly and there were only a few clouds and it seemed like a summer bank holiday. We strolled along hand in hand. Pat had remembered to bring some bread, which enabled us to feed the swans, although the ducks tried to get in on the act and were quacking furiously. However, the swans were having none of it. A duck coming in too close was in danger of getting a large peck from the swans, which obviously considered the bread to be their feast. I would have liked to get a rowing boat out but Pat was a little frightened of falling into the river so we compromised and got on the motor launch. We sat on one of the large cushions and the views from the river were beautiful. The launch pulled into the small stage. Pat and I stepped off with all the passengers and walked up the hill into the town.

We had both enjoyed ourselves that afternoon. Pat squeezed my arm and said, 'Thank you Peter, that was lovely, I did appreciate it, and I know from your expressions that you also did enjoy the day.' We caught the bus to Birkenhead, crossed the Mersey by ferry and then took the bus back and walked slowly down the avenue to Pat's father's house. Pat was fretting about her interview, which showed how much she really wanted the job. I did my best to reassure her.

On Tuesday evening, the sound of my wife singing meant I did not need to ask if she had got the new job in the department store. That night at my suggestion we walked down to the local pub, which was very nice. Pat's normal drink was egg flip, but that evening I introduced her to gin and bitter lemon as a way of celebrating her new job. Over the years Pat blamed me countless times for changing her drinking habit. What could I say?

It was Thursday night and with my case packed ready for the next day we kissed and cuddled passionately because we did not know with any certainty when I would return. I had changed to the Palm Line Shipping Company because the voyages were normally three months or less. However, even that length of time can seem an eternity if a couple are in love. The morning arrived too quickly, and with the taxi driver honking his horn, we kissed on the doorstep and said our goodbyes. I jumped in the taxi, which took me to Liverpool Lime Street Station. I was by now quite familiar with the trains to London and also the trains south-east from London to Tilbury. On seeing the *Africa Palm* for the first time after the break for leave, and my marriage, was quite different.

CHAPTER XVI

Africa Palm

The ship's routine was not new and clearly etched in my mind. It was just as well, as the Third Officer I was relieving did not know I was coming that day, but once he saw me – and after a quick hand over – he was eager to get off on leave. He had left me an unexpected present of a parrot, the relieved Second Mate's parrot that he had bought and because in Rotterdam they would not let him take the parrot off ship, I was left to look after it. The parrot was noisy and squawked almost all of the time and was often throwing things out of its cage, making my cabin a mess. It also used its beak to throw seeds all over the floor and the table. I found that at night if one covered its cage with piece of cloth, it kept the parrot quieter, allowing me to get some sleep. I found that having my radio on for a while also helped. The parrot was not sure where the sound came from.

The Chief Officer made sure that we Junior Officers supervised the loading of the cargo. I found that we were on duty from 6.30 a.m. until the dockers finished usually at 7 p.m. I was hoping to get a weekend off before we left for West Africa. However, the Chief Officer told me that the ship was going into dry dock in two days' time and that he needed us all on duty at that time. I was given a new job, one that I had not done before. I was to work or accompany the ship surveyor examining every part of the ship. My white boiler suit was not white for very long, and the comments I received were amazing such as 'Fallen down the coal hole Pete?' and 'Been along the boiler tubes you will be asking to join us engineers but not in the Red Sea.' The surveyor said to me, 'I see you have made a big hit with the crew Peter, it's made my day with all the comments.' I noticed that the surveyor's boiler suit and cuffs we immaculate, but kept quiet about it. I thought to myself if the same job came up again I would need to feel sick and be not well enough to do it. I did get to know more about the ship, however, than I did before. What good it would do me, I could not hazard guess.

After a lovely shower and checking my clothes, I found that I had forgotten to pack my uniform cap. I would need it on voyages and I would need to ask Pat to send it to me. My letter writing had diminished as I used to telephone Pat at 7.30 p.m. every other night to her friend's house. It was wonderful to hear her voice, so much more personal than letters and I felt that I could almost reach out and touch her.

Our stay in dry dock was, in fact, short. We learnt that next day we were steaming off for the start of our voyage. Up on the navigating bridge, I went to familiarise myself with everything ready for the next day. Nothing seemed out of place and I chatted briefly with one of the able seamen who was cleaning the bridge and chart room. I went down to my cabin and started writing to my wife to tell her that we were off for the hot climate of West Africa the next day.

With our guidance pilot on board we steamed out of the dock into the Thames, then steamed down river towards the English Channel. Then as the pilot came into my binoculars we moved the engine telegraph to stop, and as our ship slowed down the pilot climbed down the rope ladder, got into the launch and waved to us on the bridge. The Captain moved the telegraph to full ahead and gave instructions to the quartermaster on the wheel and away we went.

We were steaming south – or almost south – for Freetown in Sierra Leone where we had to discharge some of our cement cargo and trucks. The port routine of going up and down the cargo hatches began in Freetown. I heard on the radio that the day before there was a bad train crash and that nearly sixty people had been killed. There was virtually no breeze as the high trees sheltered us from any breeze. Captain Winter did not use the guidance of a pilot and ran the ship himself, up what were quite narrow rivers up the creek ports. It was always interesting to see an expert at work, although he told me once when I respectfully asked him that he knew the area well as he had been coming for many years. It was a pleasure to watch him work, and the way he handled the ship was nothing short of extraordinary as we could barely see the riverbanks. Even in this climate, it was possible to have fog in the creeks and on the river. Captain Winter said that one needed to have a lot of confidence in one's ability. Once up the creek ports we found it difficult to get our letters from home, which made the job harder. However, Jock, one of the engineers, had arranged a football match against an African team. I was exhausted with the heat, but despite that, we won the match, three goals to one. I reckon we were a bit lucky that day. Jock said that it was because that was our Christmas treat, even though it was coming up to the New Year. It was 6 January 1958. I asked myself where had our Christmas gone? The clock stops for no one I thought, which was just as well, because if it didn't I would still be up there in the creek ports!

We sailed next day for Lagos in Nigeria where we had to load the cargo from barges as we had to anchor in the bay. They were building a new jetty and cargo warehouse and until completed, all ships had to anchor in the bay. At least now we had a steady supply of letters from home, which helped all of us and kept us in touch with our loved ones and families.

Even though our next port of call was Freetown just a day northwards, it at least brought the ship closer to home. Some of the cargo had the name 'Dublin' on it, so we knew from that that Ireland was our first port of call close to home. One of Pat's letters had told me that she had booked a week's holiday in mid-February so I had a new target. I did not mind how long I worked for as long as we reached Liverpool by mid-February.

We had a mere seventeen days from Freetown to Liverpool via Dublin. The voyage went well with no delays and only a brief stop in Las Palmas in the Canary Islands for more fuel oil and water. We stayed in Dublin only a day and a half and steamed across the Irish Sea and up the River Mersey, passing the tall Liver Buildings. We moored swiftly at Liverpool south end docks, and when my relief Third Officer arrived after the hand over, I walked down the gangway.

This time my packing was simpler as I had been told that I would be returning to the same ship for my next voyage. It was always very nice returning to friends, and known surroundings were welcome after a good leave with my lovely Patricia. I also would be tempered to enrol for my First Mate's Certificate course at the Liverpool Technical College, which started either at the end of August or in early September. On the next voyage, Pat reminded me that I would need to begin studying again to refresh my mind. My joy in taking my leave was to return to my wife's sweet lips, which no amount of letter writing could be a substitute for. The week's leave passed swiftly and with Patricia crying softly on my shoulder, we were again saying our goodbyes.

Returning to my newly acquired friends and to the *Africa Palm* was easy. The difficulty lay in being away from my new wife, Patricia. We missed each other a great deal and had discussed my leaving the sea for a job ashore. The difficulty being was finding a job in Britain that would pay me well enough and enable me to pay the mortgage on a new home, which is what we both wanted. I had talked often with other officers not only on the *Africa Palm*, but also on different ships with similar problems. Ships' engineers could find jobs easier than us Navigating Officers, unless one took a job in piloting or work abroad supervising the loading of cargo. The sticking point for us all was that we could not leave the Merchant Navy before the age of twenty-six, otherwise we could possibly be called up to join the armed forces of the Army, the Air Force or the Royal Navy. We could each moan about the situation, but the facts would not change, so we might as well get on with what we had to do. That prompted me to dig out my study books because my next target was promotion in my current profession and that meant passing my First Mate's Examinations later that year.

We thought that the ship was fully loaded. However, we received a message from the owners to ask if we had enough space to load twenty tons of dried fish in our holds in Las Palmas. I was selected by the Chief Officer to measure the remaining space with the ship in the Bay of Biscay. I found the ladders more difficult, but the job did not take long. We called in to the Canary Islands for the dried fish as the holds had enough space to take the extra cargo. Loading took only half a day and we were steaming down to the African ports of Freetown and Lagos in the Belgium Congo to complete the discharging, then back northwards to Tiko and Calabar to load our usual logs. We had loaded the logs and had to go to Takoradi to complete loading of the cargo. We were now well down in the water and one of my jobs was to check the ship's draught, taking measurements on the stem and stern of the ship. Essentials of this nature – essentially those affecting the safety of the ship – had to be recorded in the ship's logbook, which Captain Winter ensured was done at all times. We had found, Roger the Chief Officer and I, that this time the journey home would not be as per normal because we were told that the cargo was bound for Bremen, Hamburg and Copenhagen, when instead I wanted to be relieved straightaway. However, being in the Merchant Navy, anything like that can happen, and I felt sorry for Jim as he was leaving the sea after the voyage for a shore job, the nature of which he did not tell me. I was also leaving the ship to go to the Liverpool College of Commerce to study for my First Mate's Certificate when we docked. I expected that even going to Copenhagen would not delay the ship a great deal. I had allowed more time for other delays to start at college. I was, however, anxious to see Pat for it was three months now that we had been apart.

We all felt the cold, even though it would be early spring when we reached Germany and Denmark. The heat and humidity experienced in the African ports had sapped our energy. However, it was easy to acclimatise to the cooler climate of Europe. The Continent was not what we wanted.

We wanted the ship to dock in England, in my case, if possible, at Liverpool.

In our last port, I had written to the Personnel Manager of Palm Line, a Mr Williams, to ask if I could be relieved in our first port of call at Hamburg. I also told him that I was booked into the First Mate's Certificate course at the Liverpool College of Commerce. All our cargo was loaded and we had only a few hours in Freetown to take on board fuel oil and water. Therefore, we would not need to call at Las Palmas on the return trip, for our first port in Europe would be Hamburg. This voyage was turning out to be a little different from normal as Jim, who had lots of experience, pointed out to me.

We had been away a mere eight weeks from Britain, which does not seem a long time, but when one was in love as much as I was, it was much too long. Patricia, now working in the golf department of the store, had many things to take her mind off our separation, but she expressed her loneliness in her letters.

Two weeks after leaving Freetown we would be steaming up the River Elbe to Hamburg and if my relief was waiting there I should be testing the efficiency of the German railway system! Everything went well with no delays. I was on duty on the bridge with the Captain ensuring that everyone was doing their job to the best of their ability. We stopped briefly to pick up the guidance pilot, then steamed serenely up the Elbe to Hamburg. We were lucky that day as there was sufficient room for us to berth in the dock. We moved quickly, with all the dock workers working with Teutonic efficiency. The ship was soon moored with ropes and wires just as the Captain had asked, and I was scanning the quay to see if I could see anyone with cases who could be my relief officer. He was coming to the ship in Hamburg and sure enough, I could just see a likely person waving from the quay. Naturally, I waved back, just in case I was right. For once, everything for me that day worked out splendidly.

As soon as the gangway had been put in place and the customs officers had given us clearance, up bounded the gentleman who had waved at me. He was my relief officer and we shook hands. I then went quickly through the hand over procedure. The same thing happened to some of my colleagues and we had previously discussed our route to travel together if each of us fortunately were relieved at the same moment. My bags were packed, including my study papers and several pairs of nylons for Pat. A few of us shared a taxi to the station and it was not long before we were on the train to the Hook of Holland, where we got the channel ferry to England. The weather was pleasant, as it was not nearly mid-May, and the sea relatively calm, although that did not seem to make much difference for a number of passengers who were sea sick, and quite nosily too! We, however, were used to the heavy swell and the rolling of the ship. We played cards to pass the time. Although the stakes were small, the winner made a big show as if the sums won were large. To our delight, other passengers looked at us with envy. We were, of course, all old shipmates and the talk between us was what we were thinking of doing when we got home. For my part, Pat and I had decided to go on holiday to Newquay in Cornwall, but unlike our honeymoon in St Ives, where we had booked in advance, we had decided to make a last-minute booking.

The ferry docked without us completing our card games, but our thoughts had changed from cards to getting the luggage and to completing our journeys homeward bound. I was tired and fell asleep for the remaining part of the journey by train to Liverpool. I awoke, startled when the ticket collector shouted 'All tickets please.' I gathered my thoughts and felt like thanking the ticket collector as I passed my ticket to him.

CHAPTER XVII

Home at Last, Newquay and Exams

I had dreamed of this moment for many weeks whilst at sea and I was not prepared to let it slip by. As a newly wed, the thought of holding my wife close again surmounted everything, including my tiredness. The joys were close now as the taxi turned the corner and trundled down the avenue towards the house Pat was living in. I did not have to knock at the door because Pat was there waiting for me. My telephone call from London had done the trick. We cuddled and kissed. My wife, who, of course, had got to know the new neighbours, pinched me hard and whispered to me to stop. I pretended I had not heard her, and to no avail, for Pat dragged me inside. Her dad and brothers pumped my hand and clapped me on the shoulder. They gave me a tremendous welcome, but I was eagerly waiting the time for bed with my lovely Pat.

The following day I telephoned the travel agents to see if any special offers were available for Newquay. We were indeed quite fortunate as one had a great offer if we were to book it within the week. Pat and I discussed it, but our problem was money because I had to have sufficient funds in reserve to last me for the next three, maybe four, months whilst I stayed in Liverpool and took my First Mate's Examinations.

Not being used to living ashore, Pat was by my side helping

me decide how much we would need to keep and deciding what we could afford to spend on a holiday. I knew Pat would verge on the careful side, but we decided that the holiday was worth the risk. This was to be our first holiday together since our honeymoon in St Ives by now seven months ago. We were both looking forward to the holiday. Pat had booked a fortnight off with the department store. We got the bus to the travel agents in the city centre where we signed and paid for the trip. We both thought that if the sun shone for some of the two weeks that it would be a nicer holiday than our honeymoon.

The holiday turned out to be wonderful. The small hotel-cum-guesthouse was less informal than our honeymoon hotel, but it was comfortable and pleasant with a friendly atmosphere. It was now early June and the sun seemed to realise that it was its turn to shine, and although not baking hot, it was beautiful. Pat even ventured out in her bathing costume and we could even play with the beach ball on the sandy beach, whilst the sea was almost lapping at our feet and ankles. We enjoyed ourselves each day and said to each other, 'If only we had a little bottle, we could bottle all the happiness, scenery and sunshine to bring out on a day when things were not so good.'

The holiday sped by, especially with being in love with Pat which made the holiday perfect. We were together with no one to interrupt us. We found this wonderful, but as the saying goes, 'All good things come to an end.' The next day after our travel by train we strolled down the avenues to my wife's house and, after opening the door, we took our cases inside and put all the clean clothes away. Pat gathered up the clothes that needed to be laundered and decided to do the washing the following day, Sunday. Now our holiday was over, we both had to think about going back to work. Tomorrow being Sunday, we would almost spare ourselves until Monday.

Pat threw me a pencil and pad to write down what needed to be done next week and the week after and in the near future. The list was very long. Pat took the pencil from me and scratched off half the things and put them on a smaller list. The two lists became almost the same size. Happy now, Pat gave out a sigh of relief and gave me a large smile. I then said, as Pat worked in the golf department at the department store, 'You will have to teach me how those sticks work, those that you sell.' Pat told me quite seriously those 'sticks' I was talking about were not sticks at all but golf clubs and they were expensive and way down the list of things I could afford to buy. The priority was to sort out our house and put money away for the mortgage. It was now my turn to sigh for I knew Pat was right. As we discussed often in our letters to one another, 'Money does not buy happiness – but it helps.' We were exceedingly happy at that point.

Monday came only too quickly, with Pat giving me a dig in the ribs as she was almost ready to go off to work. She reminded me that I needed to go to college to enrol and join my First Mate's course. My studying was now a priority and having done a similar course for the Second Mate's Certificate, I knew what was required of me: plenty of work studying my navigation books and learning the seaman's rules of the sea. I had at this time a new incentive because if I passed, which I must, I thought, I wanted to get a promotion. During my time at sea I had realised that having passed my First Mate's Certificate was the only way on some ships to become a Junior Officer.

Our married life went on well. We were still very much in love and had no arguments. We also went about our daily tasks. I was given the front room to study in and neither Pat's father nor her brothers disturbed me. Mind you, if I came out to watch the television it was another matter. Pat would look at her watch and would shout at me if I delayed studying for too long! The weather was pleasant and the children had begun their school summer holidays so it was a little nosier than usual with the kicking of footballs up the avenue and the playing of many kinds of games.

It was almost October now. I had been asked to do my Lifeboat Mans' Test and Certificate by rowing and sailing quite ungainly boats around the Liverpool docks. It was a diversion that in normal circumstances I would have been pleased about but this time with my exams fairly close I could have done without. I passed the sailing test, and it was back to college, desperately ensuring that nothing was missed. I had passed both the written and oral examinations and I let out a big 'whoop' with a lecturer coming out with a big grin on his face. I dashed down the road to tell Pat. She had a lovely smile and gave me a quick kiss. It had to be a quick kiss as she had customers to attend to.

My elation at passing the First Mate's Certificate lasted for a few days almost until the beginning of December 1958. After a few drinks with my friends and Pat's brothers and father, I was soon brought down to earth, looking at my seaman's discharge book to help my memory. I was given six weeks of relief jobs on various Palm Lines' ships in succession.

CHAPTER XVIII

Sailing as Second Officer

I returned to the *Africa Palm* and met many of my old friends in Hamburg. They joined the *Kano Palm* in Liverpool and after the New Year joined the *Matadi Palm* in Tilbury. In each of these ships, I was promoted to Second Officer and in February I joined the *Lokoja Palm* in Liverpool, again in my new position of Second Officer. I was on that ship until the end of August 1959, steaming twice down the usual African ports which were now so familiar to me.

Pat and I went for almost a fortnight's holiday at a property belonging to Pat's company at a small place called Odd Nee near Maidenhead and virtually on the Thames. The May weather was beautiful, as was the scenery. Seeing the wonderful Thames in all its glory makes one understand why the house prices there are so much higher than in the north. We even got a punt out on the river, not that my punting was any good, as Pat would agree as she cowered at the rear shouting at me when I accidentally splashed her.

We enjoyed ourselves and the cost was relatively small compared with our previous holidays. It was lovely to be together and away from it all. We both recharged our batteries and were both sorry when we had to pack our bags and head for the train home.

Travelling home was uneventful. We talked quietly to each other, mainly about missing one another and maybe my changing to shorter voyages. Pat was thinking about the coming winter and being in bed on her own. She felt the cold badly and without me to snuggle up to, she found it difficult to sleep.

Our holiday was soon a thing of the past once we returned to Liverpool, but it was not forgotten by either of us. Six weeks after returning a major change was put in place for Pat and I. We decided that for our happiness we could no longer be apart for three months at a time. I therefore resigned from Palm Line Shipping Company and asked to join Canadian Pacific Steamship Company and fortunately I was accepted.

After a month's leave, I was asked to join the cargo ship *Beaver Glen* steaming from London to Montreal or St Johns, New Brunswick. I had to take a small demotion to Fourth Officer, but Pat and I considered the sacrifice of seeing one another more frequently as worthwhile. The *Beaver Glen* was a fairly new ship, and once I had met my new colleagues I soon discovered those I liked. I was by that time used to meeting work colleagues on ship and I could make friends with most people.

I learnt that the winter in the Atlantic could be quite ferocious. As the ship left the shelter of the English Channel, the storm winds blew the waves and the huge swell almost enveloped us, while the spray made it impossible to see. I was on the ship's navigating bridge and had to turn on our clear view screen, so that I could then look through the screen and see the horizon. The Captain was now on the bridge standing close by me and said, 'Well, son, you are seeing the Atlantic giving you the worst of welcomes. Let's hope this weather will abate soon otherwise there will be little sleep tonight.' I nodded and said, 'Yes, I agree with those sentiments.' Just then, a huge wave washed over the ship. At that moment, I was pleased that the bridge sheltered us from the worst of the elements. However, although the storm was passing, the swell was the worst I had experienced for many years. Fortunately, the ship was not rolling but pitching heavily, making the bow almost disappear under the weight of the water. Three hours or so later at the end of my watch on the bridge and with my relief officer ready to take over his duties, the storm was already abating. I was pleased that my duties were over on the bridge that day – or night, with the sky almost black I had to peer at my watch to recognise whether it was midday or midnight!

A voice close by me reported that this was may be the last voyage up the St Lawrence River until next spring. On the *Beaver Glen* I was only the Fourth Officer and shared a watch with the Chief Officer if he did not have urgent duties to attend to. We had a long chat previously so that he knew what duties and ships I had been on and that I had a First Mate's Certificate. He treated me well and expected a lot from my previous experience. We performed well together, as the Captain had mentioned to us both earlier that day. I thought to myself that night that if I had stayed with the Palm Line and remained a Second Officer, I would have now been doing chart work and making changes on the charts from the Notices to Mariners. Every ship's Captain was sent the latest issues of the Notices to Mariners, so all the ship's charts were up to date and that all major obstructions, likes wrecks or buoys, were shown and therefore could be avoided.

Next day, with our pilot on board, we were steaming up the St Lawrence with a brief stop at Quebec City. We had little cargo to discharge there but we could clearly see the heights that our soldiers had attempted to climb during the American War of Independence. It brought back other unpleasant memories, such as when of one of our engineers had died when his clothing got trapped and the engines pulled him around. The doctor commented that he would not like anyone else to experience the sight he had seen that day.

We steamed on to Montreal and it was very cold with small snowflakes carried along by the fresh breeze. All the crew pulled on duffel coats and work gloves to give some protection from the cold. I was not used to such cold temperatures, it being a big contrast from the hot, sticky African heat I had got used to. Here in Canada the cold weather was dry and icy, and I thought it would help me acclimatise to the weather back in England, as it was almost the end of October.

Before the ship's ropes and wires were in place, the Canadian dock workers were rushing to get aboard as the gangway came lumbering down to rest on the quay. They had woollen caps and scarves around their necks and large, beaming grins on their faces, which I found to be very good news. A happy worker is usually a good worker and here in Montreal the dock workers were as good as the British ones and were used to the job they were required to do, so that little supervision was required. If they found a problem, they would soon let you know and they don't move until it was fixed, so 'Stick around mister otherwise there may be problem like a walk out.' I turned around and sure enough, it was the Second Officer speaking to me and he gave me a wink to which I smiled and waved back OK.

The cranes with their wire strops hanging were now working and lifting out the cargo from the holds. I would not have liked to antagonise the workers, and almost reading my thoughts the Second Mate said, 'Be careful what you say now otherwise things could turn out nasty.' I was glad just to keep moving around, which kept the cold out and I beat my hands together for warmth. A well-built, in fact large Canadian worker laughed and said, 'You must be new young man feeling the cold are we?' I just nodded my head and eventually he added, 'We just get used to the cold and we find it's not a problem.' The routine of discharging our cargo was now firmly established and soon it was hard to imagine anything different. Several days later, the workers were loading our cargo to return to London. Seeing me around and I seeing the same workers, we got on well, with the odd joke and smile that made the time pass more quickly. It seemed hard to believe that more than ten days had passed by and we were ready to get underway again, to steam out of the harbour and into the St Lawrence. With our pilot on board, we began our homeward journey. Soon, with shouts from the bridge to single up, and in response ropes and wires were thrown off the dock bollards, we were on our way.

My duties quickly changed to being again on the bridge as a Navigating Officer. With the Captain and pilot on the bridge along with the helmsman and I, we were now steaming towards the estuary of the St Lawrence. I overheard the Captain talking to the pilot, 'If this breeze continues it should keep the damn fog away, what do you think?' The pilot replied in a much softer tone, 'I reckon so Mister Captain.' As we steamed down the river the sun shone, though the clouds made the banks even more picturesque with the white wooden houses contrasting with the green tress and brown earth of the hills. People came out to wave. With a smile on his face, the Captain pulled the ship's whistle, which brought a nice response from the children who were waving coloured banners. Soon we could see Quebec in the distance. The pilot was ready to leave us and the pilot launch moved close alongside. Once the crew had thrown the rope ladder down for the pilot to make his descent, there was a big cheer as he climbed down, stepping nimbly onto the launch.

My memory of the voyage out of Canadian waters was still vivid and both my shipmates and I were hoping that our return to England would not be a similar experience as our outward journey. In fact, apart from the heavy swell, the weather while crossing the Atlantic was much kinder to us, with only a fresh breeze to keep the fog at bay. Fog is another pet hate of Navigating Officers. The time seemed to drag even though the weather was kinder.

I thought of Pat often and when we would dock again in London. Even though my voyages were much shorter in my present company, the schedule was not fixed. There were many things that could delay us by an extra day or two and this time I had no excuse to be relieved as soon as we docked. I was now married and several of my colleagues were in similar circumstances. Fortunately, there were no delays on the voyage home. We collected our pilot to guide us back up the Thames and with many ships passing us on their way out to sea, we continued to steam ahead into the Royal Victoria Dock in the East End and moored swiftly into our normal berth.

My disappointment was tempered with no relief officer, as the Chief Officer whispered to me 'that if all went well he would allow me to go home the next day for a maximum of two days'. On seeing my eyes light up so much, he added:

'Don't bank on it, but you can reckon that if it is possible all will be well and you will see your wife for a brief time.' All I could do was to thank him. I knew from talk with fellow shipmates that he had a good reputation as far as allowing young officers to get home was concerned, even if it was for only a day or two.

I worked tirelessly, checking on the cargo then being discharged because I did not want anything for the Chief Officer to prevent me from being allowed to be released early, even unofficially from the ship. To my great pleasure nothing prevented me and I had almost two days at home, which was wonderful for Pat and I, and we treasured that brief time we had together. We were both so pleased that my change to the Canadian Pacific Steamship Company had worked out so well and had meant being together more, even for a short interval.

My next three voyages on the *Beaver Glen* followed a similar pattern to my first. The weather in the Atlantic also decided to be kinder. The repetition of the route did not jar on my nerves even though it was no longer new to me, for being in love so much, we just wanted to see each other more often. That happened each time we made port in our usual dock, but it was still difficult to estimate exactly when I would see Pat again. When I had initially joined the ship, I did not realise that I would be on the same ship as long as I had been.

Christmas and the New Year had been and gone, and it was now almost the end of March and our Chief Officer had just told me that I was being relieved when we got into the Royal Victoria Dock. 'But where next' I thought to myself? I did not have long to wait. Little did I know that a letter was on its way to me with the answer to my thoughts.

Even my wildest dreams could not have conjured the wonderful news. A letter from Pat had arrived telling me she was pregnant and that she had been to the doctor, who had confirmed the news. We had been trying for a baby for a while, experiencing several false alarms. Now the goods news had arrived at last. Whilst at home, a letter of slightly less impact arrived informing me that I was to join the passenger liner *Empress of France* in – of all places – Liverpool, and I was to join as Fifth Officer. This was to be my first experience as a crew member of a large passenger liner. I was looking forward to the experience and, of course, the food. If the food was as nice as I had experienced on the Cunard passenger ships, then I would be in for a treat.

CHAPTER XIX

Empress of France

Joining my new ship at the Liverpool landing stage was a wonderful sensation. The *Empress of France* looked immaculate having two large funnels and it looked huge compared with the cargo ships. I was introduced to the Chief Purser and Commodore and given the once over initial inspection, along with a severe lecture on my conduct to passengers. I was also informed that my first duties would be on the gangway in my best uniform.

Meeting passengers and answering their questions and queries and passing them on to the stewards and stewardesses soon became routine. The ship not only took passengers, but also cargo and, of course, the passengers' luggage, which had to be stowed carefully.

I had a lot to learn and quickly, as one of my fellow officers explained. The passengers will expect you to know everything about the ship and he passed me his book suggesting that I read and learn everything. Once we left the harbour and before we got out to sea, I had to be able to show the passengers the boat drill, which we all had to know for safety reasons.

It was a lovely day in mid-spring as it was now the beginning of May and our first passengers were expected on the gangway. One of my fellow officers had whispered to me to go to the lower deck to be on duty at the gangway to

Painting of the Empress of France in 1960.

meet them. My uniform was inspected and I was told not to forget my instructions. I gave a curt salute and rushed down the ladders to be ready at the top of the gangway. After several hours on duty spent talking to passengers and keeping a welcoming smile, I was later informed that my duties had been performed well and where had I learned it, from other passenger ships? I just nodded, not telling them that I had watched other officers on Cunard liners, not as an officer, but as a passenger joining in New York!

It was a pleasant spring day with the sun sparkling on the River Mersey as we steamed down and out into the Irish Sea. The flags were streaming out and the ship's whistle sounded as we were on our way to Canada.

As usual, we had a short stop to allow the pilot to disembark, which he did with a wave. This was responded to by many waves from the passengers and even the Captain lifted his cap.

Despite our usual mist and fog, which meant more activity on the navigating bridge with an additional officer on radar watch, we steamed without any further delays out into the Atlantic. I soon discovered that I had been given the additional duty of inspecting the lifeboats and checking the water and stores. I had to ensure that all lifeboats were complete with baler. With more than one hundred passengers on board, I often found that the most curious passengers would enquire what I was doing. I had to be polite and sometimes humour them, which I found more difficult if I had been on duty for a long period.

As officers, we had to work long hours, sometimes if leaving port and being on cargo duty and going on watch on the bridge it could almost be eighteen hours without overtime payments. We all accepted this, although some accepted it better than others, and they complained continually. I was only twenty-five years of age at the time and reasonably athletic, so the work was not a problem for me.

I was settling in well and meeting many new people. We officers were lucky enough to eat with the first class passengers in the same dining saloon, and, of course, eating the same food, which made a big difference.

The weather was still warm, moist and sticky with a little breeze that kept the fog at bay. As we steamed up the St Lawrence to our first port of call, Quebec, I was informed that we would be there for a few hours to disembark some passengers.

The following day we steamed into Montreal where all the remaining passengers left us. I was again on duty at the head of the gangway. We had all received orders to change from our blue uniform to our tropical whites, which consisted of long white trousers. No shorts were permitted as I was told that we were not allowed to show our knees. Down in my cabin I had to find my epaulettes, which fixed onto my shirt shoulders and ensure that the buttons were on my shirt so I would pass the Chief Steward's and Commanders' inspection.

We had an afternoon free, so Pat, the Assistant Purser, and two of the lady crew, one being a stenographer, the other a hairdresser, decided to go to Verdon to the swimming pool. We enjoyed ourselves and attempted to teach one of the women to swim, but had little success as she was very reluctant to venture into the water. We were all warm from sunbathing and the cool water was very enjoyable. Pat and I enjoyed the swimming, and the time passed very quickly. I was soon reminded that I had duty to do back on the ship, so it was a mad, last minute dash as I made my farewells and hailed a taxi back to the ship, making it just in time with only a few minutes to spare.

My old ship the *Beaver Glen* was also in Montreal harbour and it wasn't long before several of my old shipmates came over to see if I had some cold beer. We chatted and they enjoyed the drinks. I was invited back to their ship the next evening. It was a bit like a stag party, with plenty of jokes being banded about, some at my expense, as I was now working on a passenger liner. 'Cargo ships not good enough for you now Pete, eh?' the Chief Officer said to me jokingly. We all enjoyed ourselves. It was a welcome break from my duties, as this did not occur very often. 'Old shipmates meeting in another port overseas, and all of us so friendly,' the Chief said to me. I could second that I thought to myself.

We found the next day that the Canadian dock workers would finish loading the cargo and the passengers would now be back on board for the homeward-bound journey. We were informed that we would steam home through the northern route via Belle Isle, which was free of ice, saving us about one hundred miles or so, which therefore meant I would see my wife earlier that I expected. Back on passenger duty, and then on bridge duties, we steamed back down the St Lawrence to Quebec, where we had some passengers to embark. We had by this time changed into our blue uniforms as we left the river and went out into the Atlantic where it would be cooler than in the shelter of the land. Nobody seemed to mind about that as we were mostly out in the open air with little shelter from all the elements.

I started to think about when I would meet up with Pat again. Writing letters to one another was not the same as holding Pat close, and with the added joy of our little baby who was on the way, life was just so wonderful that words cannot describe. In just over a week's time we would be together again. In the last letter I received, Pat had written how much she loved me and missed me, which brought tears to my eyes. We loved each other dearly and we had decided that, at the first opportunity, I would leave the sea as the threat of 'call up' was receding day by day. Once I turned twenty-six years of age I would be clear of that problem and could concentrate on thinking about a new career. At that moment, I had to put those thoughts out of my mind and concentrate on my duties on the navigation bridge.

I now had several hundred passengers' safety in my hands, which was a great responsibility, so there was no slacking or short cuts, I told myself. I had to be vigilant. We were on a

route that we had been on many times before and with
nothing in sight one still had to keep very much alert. I
suppose it is like driving a vehicle on the motorway at night.
There is not so much traffic but you still needed to keep your
wits about you.

We had left Canada in our wake, and the pilot for the St
Lawrence part of the journey had also left on his launch. As
we steamed through the moderately calm waters of the
Atlantic, the hug swell previously experienced had now
disappeared. Now, with the phosphorescence shining in the
moonlight, the bow seemed to slice effortlessly through
the water. It was a lovely feeling. A quiet night with only the
sound of the ship's engines thudding away. If Pat had been
at my side I would have had no thoughts about leaving
the Navy and nor would I wish to leave behind some of the
wonderful times and scenes that I had witnessed over the
years. This was a wonderful night, one which I would have
liked to have bottled up to bring out again to banish the bad
times of storms and heavy seas, where the ship rolls from side
to side. I am sure even the passengers must have enjoyed the
calm weather with the moonlight shining so brightly. I am
also sure many would remember the voyage for a long time
and would have probably liked to repeat it. The passengers
did not know, as many of us officers, that such calm and
placid weather was indeed a rare occasion and one was
fortunate to experience it in the Atlantic at anytime of the
year.

With a slightly daydreamy look about him, the radio
operator appeared a little disturbed, his hands running
through his tousled hair and shouting to us that icebergs had
been reported in the vicinity on the radio and also on the

route upon which our ship was sailing. Therefore, we had to keep a very careful watch and ensure that the other lookouts were vigilant. I had to whistle down to the Captain to inform him of the latest news, extra seamen were required in the crow's nest on the mast and an additional officer was placed on the bridge to ensure that an extra person was on the radar screen. It was the change that I needed to make me even more alert, although the Commander would not relish the thought of disturbing the passengers. My binoculars, which I had fixed firmly to my eyes, were scouring the horizon. Luckily, nothing was to be seen by us that night. However, it was always a reminder that nothing at sea is what it seems, as the Captain spoke into my ear, 'Don't take anything at sea for granted son.' Being ex-Royal Navy, I knew he had seen it all before and I needed to listen to what he said.

We had some warm weather, warmer than expected even thought it was now near the end of May and most people in Britain would be making plans for their summer holidays. Most of the officers and seamen would now be thinking about the return to port, and the short voyages meant that we were not away from our loved ones for very long.

Whilst on the bridge the following morning, the fog had lifted and the sunshine had disappeared. The radar scanner was circling on the mast above me and I thought I could see a smudge of something dark on the horizon. I popped into the radar screen and, sure enough, it was confirmed as our first landfall. I whistled down to tell the Captain, though only for his own interest, not expecting any action from him or needing any.

We had an Irish landfall. We had to go round Southern Ireland to get to our homeport of Liverpool. The Commander or Chief Purser in charge of the ship had the information that we had now crossed the Atlantic and land was in sight circulated to the passengers. As I looked down from the bridge, passengers in large numbers were craning their necks, some with binoculars glued to their eyes, hoping for a glimpse of Ireland. Being lower down on deck than I was on the bridge, they would be very lucky indeed to see more than a slight smudge of land.

It took us until dark, when our pilot boarded us, to guide the ship up the Mersey. Many ships were waiting at the Mersey Bar as we quietly steamed passed them. I was pleased at that moment that now any delays for me as an officer or for my first passenger liner would be minimal. We were almost moored at the Liverpool passenger terminal and my duties quickly changed from being on the bridge to standing at the head of the gangway saying goodbye to the passengers as they disembarked.

My thoughts had now reverted to thinking about seeing my darling Pat, who was now heavily pregnant with our first child. Being moored in Liverpool, I had only a short journey by rail or bus to our house in Anfield, a suburb of the city. My bags were packed and I was ready to leave the ship for, at the most, two days leave before the routine would begin again. Strange how life changes. What had been all very new to me had now become very repetitive as our ship route did not vary a great deal.

The *Empress of France* was a large passenger liner, but it could have been a ferry across the Atlantic to Canada. The weather changed a great deal with gale force winds and a heavy swell at times with infrequently calm seas and warm pleasant sunshine. However, our voyages were always short compared with my previous experiences. Montreal from Liverpool was less than three thousand miles and normally took us only seven days. Our round voyage, taking into account the time spent in each port to load and unload cargo and to give time for passengers to embark and disembark, would take us almost three weeks. Then there were hazards, of course, as the liner *Bismarck* found when it collided with an iceberg. However, none of us seaman thought much about that, perhaps being aware of the dangers kept us more alert whilst on duty.

We had a dock strike at Liverpool, for which we never discovered the reason, but it was unusual as labour relations had improved a great deal over the years. Fortunately, for our company, the dock strike had commenced when we left port and our ship was almost one hundred miles or so into the Atlantic by the time the Liverpool port came to a standstill. I found that one of my duties when not supervising the loading and discharge of cargo into and from the holds was to check the lifeboats, checking the fresh water and stores, and ensuring that all loose gear and equipment were lashed down and secure, also not forgetting to ensure that the lifeboat covers were tight when I completed my checks. In addition, every time before we left port to cross the Atlantic, I had to ensure that all the crew had security passes issued to them. This task could sometimes prove a difficult one, as some crew members had only signed on the ship at the very last minute before the ship left port.

Time had moved on, it was now July and the weather was much warmer. The Commander had issued orders to the officers to change into our white uniforms, which consisted of white shirts with epaulettes on the shoulders and long white trousers. As we steamed up the St Lawrence, I remember it being rather warm with temperatures well into the eighties. In Montreal, when having to work in full sunlight, it could get rather sticky with a high humidity factor. However, when you were as young as I was, I was twenty-five years old at that time, nothing really perturbed me except, of course, being away from my darling Pat.

Changes happened to me quickly, some I liked, others I did not. The first was promotion from Fifth Officer to Fourth Officer, and with it brought changes in my duties on the navigation bridge and my times of keeping ship watch from midnight to 4 a.m. and midday until 4 p.m., along with having the complete weather charts, mainly for passenger information. The second change affected almost everyone on ship. It was the news of a seaman's strike. Our seamen decided, despite a talk from the Captain, to refuse to work. They sat around the bow of the ship and in case of any trouble, we had extra Canadian police on board on our gangways. We also had two Canadian detectives strolling around to keep the peace.

The passengers were taken ashore and put on coaches, which took them to hotels for both lunch and dinner as we did not have the cooks or stewards to prepare and serve them their meals. The Chef Head Waiter and shore staff cooked and served the officers' and engineers' meals. The crew on strike had to make do with sandwiches and fruit. After yet another talk with the Captain, some of the crew returned to work on the ship, which meant the passengers were now back on board. We left Quebec for Montreal, steaming up the St Lawrence. The delay had only been twenty-four hours.

Worse news for some including myself was a rumour

(which had no foundation and which circulated the ship) that our destination in Britain was to be Greenock in Scotland. This involved cutting out Liverpool on the voyage home and also meant that it was now unlikely that I would see my darling Pat for another few weeks. We had no passengers on that voyage to England as we had no one to look after them. It also meant that we had the stewardesses to ourselves – for they had no passengers to oversee – and many parties were thrown and, of course, drinks abounded. Being young and red blooded, sex with the pretty stewardesses was difficult to resist although in those days sex was difficult. Even with girdles and corsets to overcome and no birth control pills available, resistance was very difficult for me to overcome. I should have been thinking about my heavily pregnant Pat, but in any case, the pretty women prevented me from being naughty.

All of my thoughts were confirmed as we crossed the Atlantic and anchored in Greenock. The passengers who wished to leave had gone ashore and were taken to Greenock. Those officers and engineers living close to Liverpool were offered nothing, so lump it we did, along with a lot of moaning.

However, getting back to writing my letters to my wife, Pat had telephoned the company and found out for herself that we were not returning into Liverpool but instead were stopping at Greenock harbour for twenty-four hours or so. What it did mean was that I received a letter from Pat with all of her news, which was wonderful. While she was heavily pregnant with our first child, I was extremely anxious that all was going well and with the enforced delay I had been making decisions about resigning from the Merchant Navy given the first opportunity. I hoped to resign by letter at the end of October, although it was just an idea not discussed or fully thought out. We had another voyage with no passengers as the seaman's strike had meant that we did not have sufficient crew to give the passengers our normal care and attention required by the company.

We left Greenock without any further delay and steamed out into the Atlantic with heavy, overcast skies looming above and a heavy swell. Perhaps it was as well that we had no passengers to worry about on that voyage to Canada, although it turned out to be incident free. We steamed up the St Lawrence for Montreal and had no delays and as we had no passengers to disembark. Therefore, as we did not stop at Quebec either, it gave us the opportunity to get to Montreal much quicker than normal.

Within a week, we were tied up at the landing stage in Liverpool. I was on duty on the stern of the ship as I caught sight of my darling Pat, standing waving madly at the ship. I waved my cap, but as she had expected to see me on the ship's navigating bridge and not being in my normal position she did not see me. As I was now Fourth Officer, my duties had changed moving into port and when departing, and this, of course, I had forgot to tell Pat.

With my decision to resign at the end of this voyage, my letters were written and posted to the company. This then was my nostalgic last voyage. My father, who had been in the Merchant Navy when I was a young boy, had been a big influence on my decision. I wanted to be with Pat, especially when our first baby was due on 25 October. Yes it was a difficult decision to resign. As I had been in the Merchant Navy for almost ten years, I knew that I would miss the many places I had visited, the companionship of the officers and the cadets who had become friends. It was particularly hard because I would miss my friends most of all. 'Join the Merchant Navy and see the world.' Well, I had seen most of the world, and I shall remember particularly New York, Montreal and Japan. It really was great looking back at my life at sea, with each day being slightly different.

I gave my goodbyes to all of my colleagues, senior officers and Captain. When I walked in and kissed my darling Pat and told her of my decision, she was amazed and enquired about my ideas of what shore job I would get and where we were to live. I told her that it would all work out well for both – all of us – and that I wanted to be with her when the baby was born. I kissed her sweet lips and gently felt her tummy, asking if the baby was moving around, to which she just nodded.

CHAPTER XX

A New Life at Home

Five days later in Broadgreen Hospital, I sat holding Pat's hand as she gripped it hard due to her labour pains. Later, I was deliriously happy to know that both mother and child were well. I felt like walking on air, wanting to shout my good news from the rooftops, as if I was the only person in the world to have a baby! Our first baby was a boy, very small and only five and a half pounds, if I remember correctly.

A new life for us all was just beginning and it would not be the same. Once the shock had evaporated, I knew that I would need to start seeking employment. I needed a position that was both satisfying and well paid. I thought that employers would be queuing up for my services after being in a responsible and well-paid position in the Merchant Navy, but as the saying goes, 'I soon had my eyes wiped.' My hunt went on for employment, with letter after letter being written to companies, but no firm offers resulted.

Christmas was soon upon us and after a wonderful Christmas together with my darling wife and new baby, and after a great party, which we had promised each other for months if everything had gone well, we now needed a babysitter for the first time. With Pat having so many aunts and cousins, we literally had people queuing to sit for us. The party went wonderfully well and after a long talk with Pat and her uncles and other relatives I received plenty of advice, some conflicting, but I was at last offered a job by a company with which I was to stay with for many years. It was called Lily Cups and Containers and made paper cups and containers, the cups used in vending machines and the containers for holding cream and yoghurt.

I started work as a Junior Estimator, and was quick to make friends with Ron, who was my senior, and he showed me what was required of me. He also introduced me to many new faces. My job was to calculate both the cost of materials and of production in the making of cups or containers and for the printing of them. The money, however, was not what I had been used to, but Pat had said that we would manage somehow. I was very disappointed also to discover that to obtain a mortgage for the house we wanted I would need to attend night school.

The next task was to cut my travelling costs to and from work, which was based in Fazakerley. A second-hand bicycle was the answer, with clothing and bicycle clips being next on the list. I was fairly trim and fit, which helped a great deal when I cycled to and from work each day. In those days, many people rode cycles and fewer people had cars, and therefore there was considerably less traffic on the roads. One day I was cycling along the road when my handle bars parted company from the rest of the bike! Miraculously I escaped with minor cuts and bruises and there was little traffic on the road.

Pat and I dearly wanted to move from her father's house and have a house of our own. We searched local estate agents and the local newspapers, *The Liverpool Post* and the *Echo*, until our eyes were sore. We had in mind the type of house we wanted while also taking into account the schools in the area ready for when our son was ready to attend.

We came across a problem. The amount of money I was earning was insufficient to meet the needs to the mortgage companies prepared to lend us the money. We were in a dilemma. Pat and I both wanted another child and having another would only add to the money problems we had. Pat was happy to have another child, despite the pain of child birth! Knowing that inspired me to work harder with my accountancy studies. We both felt that if I passed my examinations, it would help me gain promotion.

We were both delighted with the news that our second baby was on the way. Our first baby, Simon, was named after long debate and Geoffrey was to be our second son. The name chosen was a unanimous decision, again after a long debate. For a second time, Pat had chosen Broadgreen Hospital after consultation with the midwife. The birth, although still painful, was much easier second time around. Although small in stature, Pat was exceedingly brave and I was pleased that the surgeons helped her at the birth, which went wonderfully well. I was at her side as I had been previously and, thus, had seen the pain that she had to endure.

We now had two sons to look after. My decision to leave the Merchant Navy was now proving a success, for in both of our opinions, it was better if there were two parents to bring up two children. We shared the work between us. Pat showed me how to give the babies their bottles and how to change nappies. I proudly wheeled the babies up the avenue, with Pat at my side, of course. She would watch me all the time, often prompting me to slow down if she thought I was walking too quickly with the pram.

We now felt that the family was complete and our concentration reverted to the search for a different house. My studies at night school had at last brought some success as I passed the second part of the Cost and Works Accountancy Examination, which in turn brought me the promotion I had been seeking and with it a salary increase. There was joy for us both, and it brought smiles of happiness as we went to the building society with details of my new salary in the hope of obtaining a mortgage on a property.

Our searches in the local newspapers also found the house of our dreams, and it was near good schools for which our two children could eventually attend. Time had flown by, it was now August 1966, and our routine was well established. After being granted a mortgage by the building society, we moved into our new house on a Saturday. We had bought the house privately. Not going through an estate agent was lucky for us as it meant it saved us a little of our meagre resources. Savings were made too because not having a lot of furniture, we did not need a large removal van to move all our belongings. We quickly moved in and Pat soon decided that we needed some more furniture as our house – I had to admit – looked almost empty. The lounge was large with a lovely French window, which opened out on to the garden.

Pat, who knew where all the best Liverpool furniture shops were, soon found a three-seat lounge suite that was considerably reduced as it was apparently 'shop soiled', although to my eyes it looked perfectly good. We purchased it and it was delivered the following week. It turned out to be a very good purchase and lasted us over twenty-five years, only having it re-covered once, at Pat's insistence, to match the new colour décor.

Our eldest son, Simon, liked his new school, Hudson Primary School, which was very handy. It was no more than four hundred yards from where we lived, with no major road to cross, but Pat still insisted on walking him to school each morning and meeting him at the school gates at the end of each school day. The school was also attended by Geoffrey and was excellent.

For my part, my new route to Fazakerley was worked out carefully and I ensured my bike was checked out each weekend ready for the Monday morning. My friends and colleagues gave advice on which route was best, what to watch out for and to be most careful about.

My slight apprehension at leaving the sea behind and being afraid of potential boredom with a life on shore had now disappeared. There was much to do and my life was hectic: helping Pat with the two children, studying for my accountancy examinations and, of course, my work, which never seemed to be the same for two days running.

My failure at my accountancy exams, however, was much to my horror, but my dismay was soon forgotten. My company was part of a large group and needed companies to install computer systems of a similar type, for both accountancy and personnel. They needed a person in each of the companies within the group to be trained in all computer systems used and be appointed to the position of Systems Co-ordinator. I had been studying and attending night school. The company accountant called me in and asked if I wanted to study computers instead of continuing my accountancy studies. However, in those days, computers were fairly new to most of us, and being having potential and receptive to changes at work, I agreed to take the position. The decision brought with it another huge change in my life. I had to study some more about Organisation and Methods, as this was a prerequisite to becoming a systems person in our company and to being a Systems Co-ordinator.

My ambition was now spurred on by the thought of more money to spend on my family and, of course, to pay the mortgage. My life was now so full of things to do that I would not have believed it possible a few years earlier.

Our two sons and Pat also needed my attention besides my new career. My old life in the Merchant Navy was well and truly a part of my past. I encouraged my sons to keep a balance between studying and being out with friends, not forgetting their sports activities, which they were both very keen on. Both boys had a healthy appetite and knew the necessity for study, and with the three-year age gap between Simon and Geoffrey, it gave Geoffrey the competition to match his elder brother in almost everything they did.

Pat and I had little trouble from either of our sons. They were both very aware that their father still attended night school and it brought home to them the importance of school studies. I think I was probably going to be their competition a few years time! This was a pleasant thought for me as it was for them, as I was not only their father, but also an incentive in the real world in which they were growing up into.

Pat commented to me one day that now that both boys were at school, she was becoming a little bored at times and asked if I minded if she took a part-time job in the local post office. We discussed this at great length and agreed that if that was what she wanted to do, then I had no objections at all. I agreed that whatever money Pat managed to earn was hers to spend on whatever she liked.

The post office was only about one hundred yards away from the house and the owner, unbeknown to me, had already offered Pat the position if she wanted it! He knew we had two young children and agreed that if the children were taken poorly or during the school holiday, he would do his best to allow her the time off. As the school was not far away, the children knew where their mum worked as they often brought sweets from the post office with their pocket money. It was a perfect arrangement. Working part-time stopped Pat becoming bored and meant she got out to see people and gave her money to spend on clothes or on the boys. They always needed new clothes or shoes as they were both growing up fast.

My thoughts now turned to me buying a second-hand car, which would enable us to visit my mother and sister in Lincolnshire. Pat advised me that her Uncle Frank was probably the best person to seek advice from when buying a used car. He was very eager to show me around cars, and it wasn't too long before we purchased a nice looking Ford Popular, which we kept in the family for many years. I had already been taking driving lessons and I had passed my test, albeit at the second attempt. After paying for the car insurance and obtaining a licence, we were all set for a new adventure. My cycling days were now over, although I kept the bicycle and occasionally used it on nice sunny days. Riding kept me active and cost nothing to get to work. I let the weather forecast make up my mind on whether I should cycle to work or leave the bicycle in the shed.

We had a different sort of adventure when we decided to go for a day-trip to North Wales. I was well aware that we did not have a great amount of petrol, but I was a bit surprised as we tried to motor up what seemed like a rather steep hill and the engine cut out. Being new to cars and looking at Pat's face, I realised I needed to do something quickly. I quickly put on the brakes and also put large boulders behind the rear wheels of the car to prevent it from rolling backwards. As I had an empty can in the boot, I quickly set off in search of fuel. I was lucky. The nearest petrol station was not too far away and when I explained the situation the man in the petrol station said that he wished he had £5 for every time somebody had said the same! He went on to explain that the car we owned had a gravity-feed system, unlike more up-to-date models which had electric petrol pumps. I remember walking back up the hill very red faced with a can full of petrol. My red face was caused by exertions and was also due to being a little embarrassed at my failure to ensure we had sufficient fuel.

I was slowly learning that the joys of driving the car were sometimes not as pleasant as I had imagined. It climbed sluggishly even the smallest of hills, as I found out by motoring over the Pennines to visit my mother and sister in Lincolnshire. I frequently used my arms – this had been pointed out by my sons – in an attempt to help the car up the gradient. It was frustrating as larger lorries we had past earlier waved as they chugged past. It was like something out of a 'Carry On' film, which was not always funny for me at the time.

The incident of running out of petrol gave Pat and the boys plenty of fun at my expense, and they constantly reminded me when the petrol gauge was below half full. Fortunately, being constantly reminded, we never ran out of petrol again.

Motorways in those days were still only ideas on a drawing board or were in at the planning stage and not yet common especially in the east–west direction across the country. Many with good memories will say 'What about the M1?' I know it went north–south but I cannot recall using it, certainly not in my early days of motoring.

Our life began to take on a fairly routine pattern with work and two nights a week at night school, which were often very rushed. The Liverpool College – which I attended for a long time when I was in the Merchant Navy and then later when studying for my accountancy examinations – had now become almost a part of my life. I was now studying Organisation and Methods (O&M), which showed me how best to help set up procedures in the office which gradually helped the way in which we all worked. Passing my exams in O&M was just the beginning. Next, I was studying and learning about computers, often going away on courses, which meant leaving Pat and my sons.

Pat was a wonderful wife. She never once complained about my being away from home and having to look after the boys on her own. We both knew that I was only away reluctantly to enable me to complete my studies, which meant I could progress to the position of Systems Co-ordinator.

The course on computer system analysis and learning about payroll systems, at that time they were manual systems. I was then asked by the company accountant to examine a way to introduce a computer payroll system, which I did, and we installed a computer printer and computer terminal where we coded up the relevant information. I looked after computer systems and trained up two or three staff to input the data onto magnetic tapes. The data were then transmitted by telephone each week to the central computer in the Bristol headquarters.

With my new found skills in O&M and my knowledge of computers, after a long discussion with Pat, I decided to move to another company. The decision was a hard one for me to make as I had made some very goods friends at work. At lunchtimes, we would play chess and cards, and not forgetting the jokes which kept us in frequent laughter. In fact, little did I know at that time that we would all keep in touch and meet on a yearly basis, usually around November each year. The factory producing paper and plastic cups and containers was close to the Aintree Race Course, which is famed for the Grand National. Sadly, the factory has now been closed for several years.

CHAPTER XXI

A Fresh Start

My decision to move to yet another company, the largest manufacturer of lifts and escalators in Britain, was in hindsight a wise one. Therefore, if you want a good lift, not only in spirit, but also body and soul, then Otis is the name to remember. The new company, which was fairly close and only about a mile further from my home, was to be part of my working life for many years. I was made most welcome as an O&M Analyst, although my new colleagues were mainly Computer Programmers, Computer Operatives and Systems Analysts. Jokes, of course, were quickly made at my expense: 'Counted any pencils today, Peter?,' they would say. I soon found out that being an O&M person could be improved upon as I was a one-man band with no one working with me. However, this did not last long as within a year I was transferred to the position of Junior Systems Analyst, the jokes slowly ceased! We had our own computer at the Otis factory and computers became a way of life. I continued to learn about every aspect of my new company.

Life at home was mixed, and both Pat and my two sons were happy. I expected I would have a quiet life away from work, but this was not to be. My sons joined the Scouts, albeit at different times due to their age gap. Eager to help them, I enjoyed sport of most kinds, especially football. I became the 'football man' with a car full to bursting with

Working at a computer terminal as a
Systems Analyst at Otis Elevators.

boys who had to be taken to football pitches all around the area. Sometimes if we were short of players, I would drive around with my excited sons giving me directions to houses of boys who might like to play until we had a complete team.

As mentioned earlier, neither of our sons needed much coaxing to do their homework, with my eldest, Simon, setting a good example to Geoffrey. They both did well at school and thankfully continued to do well in their studies and, although not perfect, they were not cheeky children. I tried not to be an interfering father, although I felt that my decision to be at home with Pat and help look after my boys was a wise one. I still feel that a family needs a balance from both parents because all mothers have a hard time washing, ironing, cooking and cleaning, and keeping the house tidy. There are many little things that we men do not even think about, unless, of course, they have to do the tasks themselves.

Our holidays in the early days were never forgotten, these always being in Britain. Caravans and small but usually friendly bed and breakfast and evening meal establishments were at that time the best we could afford, but we always had a lovely time, except for when the weather was not too kind. We were often very lucky with the weather, however, a particular favourite holiday destination of mine being Cornwall. It had lovely beaches and the surf for my sons was good. Foreign holidays were only still a far off dream and still for the rich. And at that time, there were other more important and pressing needs.

My work was hard but interesting. I was still learning about computer systems and I found that installing a new computer payroll system meant trips to Peterborough to learn at first hand about the payroll packages from the designers of the system. From what I can recall, once installed complete with a personnel package computer system attached, it worked very well and lasted the company many years. It was one of my best choices of a package system I made and it was interfaced with our own 'in house' system with written time and attendance programs. What with my work and going on regular computer courses, the time flew by and although my family life was quieter, the demands on my time were more pleasant. I was still very much in love with Pat and now with my hard work and my promotions we had considerably more money to spend. This, in turn, led to many exciting opportunities, such as going on our first continental holiday, not flying but a longer journey. I boarded the coach in Liverpool with my wife and youngest son Geoffrey and the journey proved to be long and very tiring, but a new experience for us all. We reached our mobile home in the South of France before lunch the following day and a lovely warm sun greeted us.

Geoffrey reminded me recently that our holiday in France was not our first holiday overseas. However, it was the first holiday we had to the Continent by coach and it is the one that sticks in my memory. It also showed me how many people Pat knew, for she was familiar with several people on the coach, apparently because they all lived relatively close to us. Once in France we visited several places I had only just heard about recently such as Monte Carlo and the yacht basin, which berthed the most beautiful yachts and had many rich people all in their finery reclining aboard their magnificent boats. You could almost smell the money. It really was a sight to behold. I know I stared impolitely, I suppose wishing enviously at what I would like to have been able to afford their yachts, clothes, jewellery and also the sight of the lovely women. It was only a dream as Pat tugged my arm for us to return to our coach. Also as a motor racing fan, only being able to watch the major motor races on television, it showed me how difficult it must be to drive a racing car around the streets of Monte Carlo.

The next event that I recall from our holiday was a wonderful party we attended on the mobile home site to celebrate a royal event. Pat and I went to the local super-market and purchased a bottle of white rum, which was reasonably price. That should have told me something, but it did not, and the bottle of spirit made all those who drank it pretty drunk! Even mixed with cola the rum was potent. Those people on the site that we had got to know would have in normal circumstances remained quite demure, but now they were dancing and singing. As somebody said to me, 'Your drinks made the party go with a bang.' It sure was some celebration.

The next day was a different matter. Everyone I saw was holding their heads, and putting their fingers to their lips for people – and their children – to keep the noise down. The most that was said was, 'Where are the headache tablets or does anyone know a cure for a hangover?' Many people had different ideas that were bandied about, but most without success. Pat gave me some stick after that for suggesting she try something different from her normal egg flip or gin and bitter lemon. Being a trier, Pat drank the Bacardi and coke, which she began to enjoy, but the white fire rum was a different matter. Looking back on it now, I should have kept the empty bottle so as to know what to stay clear of in the future. Geoffrey must have thought us adults as crazy at our antics as he did not drink anything other than soft drinks and iced water. At the party, people who neither of us knew soon became our friends. It was a wonderful way to break the ice, but it is not to be recommended for its after events and the hangovers it created.

The holiday came to an end far too soon for us all. None of us spoke a word of French but Geoffrey had to be prised apart from his new French girlfriend. When the coach was about to depart he was still kissing and cuddling her amongst the chorus of wolf whistles from the coach passengers. Both Pat and myself remarked that it would be wonderful if we could have bottled up all our happy events to bring out later on dull or sad days. Twenty-four hours or so later, we all uncoiled ourselves from the coach, thanking the driver as we departed, and collected the luggage. I think that after a holiday as good as that one turned out to be we were all ready to get back to work and our normal everyday routines.

CHAPTER XXII

Work and the Family

Time moved on after the holiday to France. Geoffrey became the Casanova of the family, which he obviously enjoyed. Both our sons despite their studying for 'O' and 'A' Levels were keen on sport and playing football for the school and any other free time they had they played for their local teams. In the summer months it was tennis, where they left me way behind. I was not good enough to give them a hard game. My work and the computer courses, however, did not allow me much time to spend with the boys during the week, but I spent time with them during the weekends.

Simon was intent of his examinations and he got the grades he required in his 'A' Levels to qualify for university. Next, it was which university would offer him a place. He eventually chose Loughborough and, of course, I influenced him to try a course in Computer Technology. We knew that we would both miss him, but we were very proud that he was going to his chosen university.

Once away at university he telephoned home each week. Naturally, we were greatly concerned when we did not receive a call for over two weeks. Pat was extremely distraught and we tried in vain to contact him. We eventually received a telephone call from him and he informed us that he was leaving the course, as most of the other students had studied for 'A' Levels in Computer Science and he felt he was being left behind. He kept us in suspense for several minutes before he informed us that he was accepted on the Economics course, although it did not commence until September of the following year. I had to drive to Loughborough to collect Simon and all his belongings. I can recall the car being piled high with his books and clothes.

That year was especially good for all of us. Simon wrote off and telephoned around until he managed to get a job in a large insurance company near Pier Head in Liverpool. Pat continued working in the local post office, which she enjoyed, and Geoffrey was studying for his 'A' Levels. I was continuing to learn new computer skills and made several visits to Peterborough to attend training courses, mainly about the theory and practical application of the payroll system. It was an enjoyable time for me, meeting many new people and learning about and discussing their jobs and the work they did within their company, and also what salaries everyone was on.

The Payroll Manager was very experienced and was most interested to know the differences that would apply to his staff from his current system. We began to print all the factories' payment slips on the new system. It proved very successful and with the new time and attendance system, all went very smoothly. I continued to support this and other computer systems throughout my career with Otis Elevators. My training in accountancy many years before had stood me in good stead with our payroll and similar systems and assisted me in talking with senior people in the organisation.

While at Loughborough Simon joined the OTC (Officers Training Corps) and he is the kind of person who does not believe in doing things by half. He initially joined for the extra money, even though I gave him a monthly allowance through a covenant (which the Tax Office provides). After a short while he soon found himself helping to run several OTC centres.

After taking a year out, Simon returned to Loughborough. Geoffrey had got five 'A' Levels and was off to Trent Polytechnical College in Nottingham where he was to study Accountancy and Finance. Both sons were away from home at the same time, thus leaving Pat and I at home on our own. We had to be prepared to man the telephone if either son was need of us, and I was the taxi driver, taking their belongings from place to place as the need required.

Both Pat and I were extremely proud in July 1983 when we went to Loughborough University to see Simon graduate and receive his Bachelor of Science in Economics. He then went on to join Rolls Royce in Derby and ended up sharing a flat with Geoffrey in Nottingham.

Geoffrey had followed his brother and joined the OTC, mainly, I think, for the chance to go skiing, and it was not long before he was off to Scotland with the OTC. He took to skiing like duck to water. He was a natural, although I am led to believe that the ski instructor was superb. Both Simon and Geoffrey, however, were very fit and active, which helped tremendously in their trips with the OTC to Germany, Austria and Cyprus.

Again, Pat and I were extremely proud when Geoffrey qualified in the Chartered Institute of Management Account (CIMA). We were over the moon that they had both done so well. As parents, we may not have expressed our delight sufficiently at their wonderful achievements. However, I may have said to them well done and that they needed to put their qualifications to good use now.

Geoffrey also followed Simon to Rolls Royce for a while. He was also sponsored by the company to continue his college studies. Geoffrey started to play rugby for the company too, which he still continues to do to this day. He has also played for Hemel Hempstead and has played semi-professional rugby league.

On obtaining his degree, Simon left the OTC and joined the West Mercia Territorial Army Regiment, rising up the ranks as a part-time soldier to Second Lieutenant, then First Lieutenant, then up to Major. At that stage he was working hard for Rolls Royce, and what with travelling from place to place with the OTC, he began to find it too much of a burden and was forced to resign from the Territorial Army regiment.

Pat was now being asked by the owner of the post office and shop if she would be willing to open the shop up one day a week. This was discussed and agreed and it became part of her weekly routine. She had to be up by 7.00 a.m. each Wednesday to get the papers ready for delivery and also for those calling into the shop on their way to work – I expect those working maybe an early shift. Although Pat enjoyed meeting people, she was not too keen on leaving the house so early. People still come up to me now and say that they miss her happy smiling face and cheerful manner.

As my progress continued year after year, my salary also gradually increased, giving us more money to spend on holidays. We could now book foreign holidays on a regular basis. I don't think they was anywhere in Europe we have not visited. We also had more of a chance to go out and soon got into a routine of going out every Saturday evening, which we both enjoyed tremendously. For many years, we met up with friends at the St George's Club in Maghull, where we enjoyed good entertainment and could dance.

This became the highlight of our week. We did not drink excessively but nevertheless had an enjoyable night out. We noticed as the weeks went by that the numbers attending the club were getting less and less, and it wasn't long before we were informed that the club was to close. We had now become very friendly with a couple, Elsie and George, and they persuaded us to join The British Legion Club and we have never looked back since. Without a shadow of doubt, it was a good move.

Both our sons felt that a change was needed in their careers. Geoffrey moved to a company in Uttoxeter, Staffordshire, called Elkes Biscuits, which is part of the Northern Foods Group. Simon moved to an engineering company and immersed himself swiftly into the technology of production of manhole grids and other similar products. As years go, 1988 and 1989 were good for all of us. We all progressed with our lives and it could hardly have been described as boring. Unfortunately, my memory lets me down time and time again, but if I was to say why it would mar the remainder of my story.

'Casanova' Geoffrey was caught at last by Lynne. They lived together in Derby for a short time before moving to North London. He had again moved positions, but still within the Northern Foods Group, working as a Financial Controller for a company called Panificio, a bakery that produced speciality breads based in Wembley. On 16 October 1992, Sophie Elizabeth Embley arrived weighing in at a healthy seven pounds twelve ounces. Both Pat and I were extremely pleased, especially Pat who had longed for a daughter herself, but our two boys had been quite enough. Sophie was a pretty little baby and because of the long distance between us – London to Liverpool – we did not see as much of them as we would have liked.

Simon also changed his job – still in the vicinity – to another engineering company, which made many things, but the main products were cast-iron grids used by councils. He made the move into purchasing and within a short period was promoted to Purchasing Manager. Simon was never content in his work unless it gave him the challenge that he and our family seem to need. He found out about all aspects of his firm and about the manufacturing process, and also travelled to many parts of the world including Russia. A change of jobs into insurance came next. This time it meant a change in location and he joined Norwich Union where he relocated from Nottingham to live in Norwich.

Simon, who married Sara, brought a family home with a large garden. His year at Eagle Star Insurance in Liverpool must have stood him in good stead for the new job. In recent years Norwich Union has been involved with another major large insurance company and the joint insurance company, I am told, is now the largest insurance company in Britain. Currently Simon is a Director. On trying to congratulate him, Simon is the master understatement. He told me he wasn't on the board yet, and with the merger, who knows? He didn't seem at all worried about the amount of work ahead of him. The merger will leave the company with far too many senior staff and several people will have to reapply for their own positions, and may have to relocate to new positions, even new locations.

My achievements are put more into perspective when I compare them with what my sons have achieved. Although computers are now part of everyday life, I was still learning the application I was installing into the new computer system. I had to take care and learn everything exactly as I had been shown and told because I had to tell many others the differences between the new system and the old. The computer courses were a great help to me. As my company expanded, I found myself visiting difference offices, which took me away from home for short periods. I was having to leave home at 6.00 a.m. to drive to Hull. I found with the motorways close to my house that I could get to the Hull office before most other employees had even arrived! I found the work interesting because I had to be polite and explain and answer any questions and try to ensure that all I told them was fully understood. I tried to keep things as simple as possible and not make the new systems seem any more difficult. I had to stress that the interfaces to the existing systems would make life much easier once fully understood.

At the end of each night, I had to book into a boarding house because it was too far to drive back and forth each day. The telephone again became the only contact between Pat and myself. She did not like me going away and only being at home at the weekends. It was good she had the part-time job to stop her from becoming too lonely. The compensation, however, was the monetary rewards. We had more foreign holidays and found that we could look through holiday brochures without spending too much time and not having to worry about the cost.

Pat was always very careful and on guard about what we spent and everything was kept within budget. She would often remind me of what we previously could afforded, and it was a good reminder to keep me in check, for which I have since been very grateful. This kind of check only inspired me to work harder. We discussed everything and seldom argued. I was beginning to see everything clearer now and I realised how hurtful my absence was to Pat, although she never once complained. We had a true partnership. I loved Pat and that after being together for so long it was wonderful.

As my company head office was in London, I was now being asked to spend more time there. I had to document all our computer systems so that the document could be self-explanatory to another company, which had been contracted to provide computer support for all the systems. I had to be on hand to answer any queries that might be required by staff not familiar with our systems. The next request was that I move to London on a temporary basis. Pat agreed, so it was not long before I took on a new routine. Each Monday I would get a train to London with a colleague, Don, whom I shared a flat with, and at the end of the week did the reverse journey to Liverpool. Don and I got on well and we both got used to the London Underground system, which we used to get from the flat to the office on a daily basis.

In the evenings on returning to the flat, we worked out a cleaning rota to ensure that the flat was kept clean and tidy. I wouldn't say it was spotless, but it was adequate for two men. We even ended up doing the shopping on a rota, and going for a walk when the chores were completed. We soon got to know the best places to buy food and where to go for a drink, although neither of us were heavy drinkers. This pattern continued for sometime and from what I can recall and talking to people, it must have gone on for longer than I thought.

Reading a current letter from Bill, who was the Manager of the Computer Department in London, I was amazed that I provided support for the systems up until 1996. How time flies, especially when you are enjoying it and working with so many knowledgeable people, some of whom became friends not just colleagues.

Upon consultation with Pat, it was decided that I should take the early retirement package, which was offered me. It was a difficult decision, if I remember correctly, the main reason being to avoid the travelling and be at home with Pat. Pat was by now suffering severely with arthritis and found everyday chores increasingly difficult to cope with. Although she never complained, I could see that just keeping the house clean, opening jars, peeling potatoes and so on was causing her considerable pain. Therefore, in March 1998, I joined the ranks of the non-working retirees.

CHAPTER XXIII

Retirement and Another Life

We decided to redecorate the house to Pat's liking and got the garden ship shape, the lawns trimmed and mowed. It was then time to look for a holiday! We had been lucky to have holidays around many parts of the Mediterranean, but this time I wanted to celebrate my retirement and our Ruby Anniversary (forty years married). To do this we booked a cruise with one of the largest holiday companies. Speaking to many people anxious to give us advice as this was our first cruise, they advised us that we needed clothes for every occasion. Fortunately, I am still slim, and Geoffrey gave me his dinner suit that no longer fitted him, but which fitted me like a glove. I was glad I took it with me as we had our photograph taken with one of the senior officers and were all dressed up for the occasion. The cruise was a wonderful holiday. It brought back memories to both Pat and myself and we enjoyed the new life on board the cruise liner.

The weather was also kind, and our trips ashore and the scenery were often spectacular. Many places were new to us both although some places we had visited before. They looked so different from the sea with the sun gleaming on the water and the hills and the white-washed buildings on the coastline. In the smaller ports, we had to step aboard a small launch – the *Sapphire* – to reach the shore and see the places we had not visited previously. We were fortunate for the sea was calm, otherwise I think Pat would have given it a miss, although it was late summer and the weather was still very hot.

Some of our fellow passengers were mopping their brows whilst others had small battery-operated fans. Both Pat and I enjoyed the heat, and given the slight breeze we found it pleasant. The breeze was warm unlike the cold winds that we have in Northern England. Seeing the beautiful liner, all the local traders thought we had loads of money to spend so their prices were high. We soon got used to the idea and thought of bartering for any goods we wanted, very often getting the price down by half of what was originally asked. Cafés and restaurants were different, however. You had to pay the prices unless you had both the time and inclination to search for something cheaper. Pat and I were sorry when one of the ship stewards told us we were heading back to England. Looking at the sun and being an ex-Navigation Officer, I knew which way our passenger liner was heading, the steward had just confirmed my thinking.

One of the officers asked if we would like to visit the bridge. Pat declined the offer, shaking her head. I on the other hand jumped at the chance. Upon arrival on the bridge, I was shown all the modern equipment. I marvelled at the easy way of finding the ship's position using satellite navigation. When I explained to our guide officer that unless we were in sight of land we had to use sextants to shoot the sun, he laughed and commented on how things had changed. Our cruise soon ended but as the saying goes, 'All good things come to and end.' We joined the queue to leave the cruise liner and it was not long before we were homeward bound.

The unexpected does sometimes happen to all of us. Mine was an unpleasant experience and in someway I am fortunate that I do not remember anything of it. Simon told me that we, that is Pat and myself, were travelling to Norwich to visit him and Sara and their son, James, when on the Sleeford Road not too far from Newark on a blind bend our car collided with a lorry. The lorry was carrying a load of logs. Pat was killed in the accident and I only just survived. None of this I remember, not even today. I was taken to Grantham Hospital and then transferred to the Queen Elizabeth Hospital in Birmingham. The facilities at the Queen Elizabeth were apparently better for people who had sustained head injuries.

My first memory is a brief one. It took place in the Norfolk and Norwich Hospital where I had been transferred to and where my son and his wife told me that Pat had died. I had not been told the news before as the doctors thought it might delay my recovery. The magnitude of the disaster did not sink in straightaway. My brain was confused. I had been told that Pat's funeral had been arranged and taken place in Maghull where we had lived. Thinking back, it must have been dreadful for Simon and Geoffrey to have to arrange their mother's funeral whilst I lay in hospital not knowing whether I would survive. Once the doctors were certain that I would live to fight another day – not their words but mine – I was transferred to a rehabilitation unit, St Michael's Hospital, near Norwich. My next memory was being asked by one of the staff at St Michael's what my hobbies were. I remember saying gardening and also that one of the male staff's eyes lit up. I quickly realised why he also smiled enthusiastically. I was taken by the arm and pointed to the gardens and given the task of weeding the wheelchair flower beds ready for planting the spring plants! I started off in a wheel chair and then progressed to crutches as my balance had been severely affected by the accident. I found that working out in the open air of the gardens and being a bit rebellious – not to mention that I found the crutches difficult to cope with – I hid the crutches behind the wardrobe in my room. My balance was improving daily and when asked where my crutches were, I slurred my words, deliberately making myself mumble. Not being able to understand me, the staff watched carefully and being able to get around without falling meant that nobody mentioned the crutches again.

St Michael's Hospital was, I suppose you could describe, a little like a mansion house. It was set in idyllic surroundings up a long drive from the road. It was so very quiet with gardens and grasslands surrounding the buildings. Looking after the gardens became a full time job for me, which I enjoyed. I often went with some of the staff to the local garden centre where we purchased many spring plants and I also got some tomato plants. On our return, I would spend the majority of the day planting. With the help and assistance of one of the experienced gardeners employed by the hospital, we planted the tomato plants in large tubs in the greenhouse. The weather in Norfolk during the spring was warm with the sun shining most days. The tomato plants needed regular care and attention with watering and feeding regularly.

I was always an early riser, and the staff soon became aware of this. My breakfast things were always left out ready for me. This enabled me to have my breakfast before any other patients had stirred.

Simon my son and Sara visited me regularly. On one occasion, Simon drove me to the small market town of Aylsham as I was running short of cash. On arriving at the cash point machine, I inserted my bank card only to find that it was retained. I am not sure whether I typed in the wrong PIN number in or what I did. With the banks closed over the weekend, Simon suggested that I telephoned the bank on the following day to sort out the problem. I did just that and was told by them to write giving details and a new bank card would be issued to me. On completing the letter and getting it ready to post, I found I had no postage stamps. I asked a member of staff where I could purchase some stamps and I was told that I needed to go into the post office at Aylsham. I was also told that I could not leave the hospital grounds without a member of staff (I had to be accompanied at all times) but that due to a staff shortage at present, there was no one available to accompany me. This frustrated me greatly as I wanted a stamp to post the letter.

The following morning was glorious and being an early riser, I had breakfast before anyone else had started to stir. I then decided to walk out the back way and go into Aylsham alone to get the stamps and to post my letter. The nearest town was about one mile way, and what with working in the garden, I was physically fit and with the sunshine it was a lovely, warm early morning. The footpaths were quiet and I enjoyed the walk. I soon found the post office and bought the stamps, allowing me to post the letter to the bank. I ventured into another shop and was having a look around when I was tapped on the shoulder. I recognised the person as a nurse from the hospital. She asked if I had permission to be out on my own, and on shaking my head she just glared at me and ordered me to get in her car.

Whilst she drove me back to hospital, she explained that one of the reasons why I needed permission to leave the hospital was that all patients had to be accounted for in the case of an emergency such as a fire drill. If I was not accounted for, they might assume that I was in the hospital buildings and a fire-fighter could risk his life to search for me. I cowered in the car seat and apologised profusely and tried to explain my reason for going into town. I thought about how selfish I had been and what a stupid act I had carried out, and that I should not do it again. Two or three weeks later, however, it was a lovely day and being frustrated at staying within the hospital grounds I again went for a walk into Aylsham, only to be spotted again by the same nurse! This time she was extremely annoyed and I got a severe ticking off. She was really quite angry as she explained that she would have to complete a lot of paperwork on my behalf.

The days went by and I tried to keep my head down. Simon arrived one Sunday in his pink German Porsche and tapped on the dining room window as we were just finishing lunch. He said he had come to take me swimming with James, his son, and that he had a pair of swimming trunks for me. I did not really want to go but felt I couldn't really refuse after he had taken the time and made such an effort. We sped off and within half an hour arrived at the swimming pool, which was somewhere along the east coast. Before my accident, I had been a reasonable swimmer, but this time I found it very difficult even to perform the smallest of strokes. My grandson James, however, was throwing small disks into the water and retrieving them very quickly, obviously having a wonderful time. Simon watched me like a hawk. My swimming was poor but I enjoyed the event, something that I would have not thought of trying myself.

The following weekend Simon suggested that I spend the weekend at his house with Sara and James and, of course, a sporting activity was arranged. Both of my sons are very sports minded. This time it was to be a round of golf. Simon had arranged a motorised golf buggy, which he drove. He said he wanted to play eighteen holes, hence the buggy, as I would not have been able to walk the distance. It took me a long time to play and it was well over twelve months since I had played last. Simon drove the buggy, which he insisted I sat in, right up to my ball and if I got off sooner than instructed he yelled at me. I did show some signs of improvement towards the end of the game. It was a long day, though very enjoyable and memorable for me. On the Sunday, Sara asked if I would like to attend church with her for the Mothering Sunday Service. Simon was busy working from home and was unable to attend, so I acted as the absentee father for the morning. James was in one of the choir stalls and was chosen to say a prayer, which he did well. I was most impressed.

Geoffrey also invited me to stay at his house for the weekend and we went to the Derbyshire Dales for the day along with his wife, Lynne, and their daughters, Sophie and Eliza. It was a very hot and sunny day and we took along a picnic. We crossed a river via stepping stones and I was well protected by Geoff as we crossed. On getting back to the house, I was extremely tired. It must had been the fresh Derbyshire air and perhaps the physical exercise which I found harder than I would like to have admitted at the time. Sophie and Eliza were more adroit that I. Lynne told me that they very often went walking and I must admit I can understand why. The scenery was magnificent.

As usual, I wanted to do what I did before the accident. The accident had left me more impulsive and I very often paid the price for my impulsiveness. Whilst at St Michael's I had been asked to attend two case conferences. This, provided I followed the hospital rules, led me to believe that I would be discharged soon. At the last conference they decided I could leave provided that I had twenty-four-hour care. Both Simon and Geoffrey looked into several options. Nursing homes were one option, and these were looked into in Norwich, Derby and Liverpool. On seeing several, I decided that this was not the route I wanted to take. I was asked where I wanted to live when I was finally discharged and I had decided that I wanted to return to Liverpool.

Simon took me back to Liverpool for a weekend stay in the house I shared with Pat for many years. Little did I know that whilst visiting Liverpool, Simon had been in contact with the Rathbone Rehabilitation Brain Injury Centre which we visited and where we met some of the staff. The centre at the time was full. However, it was prepared to accept me once a bed became available. I was impressed by the centre, a feeling I conveyed to Simon, and I said that I was prepared to go on the waiting list. Simon then talked with the staff and it was expected that a vacancy would probably become available around August.

We returned to St Michael's where I constantly badgered staff with regards to any news received about my transfer to the Rathbone Brain Injury Centre. All I got was shakes of heads. This period was not good for me. I was frustrated. I did not want to be at St Michael's any longer and as the end of

August was almost upon us, there was still no word of a transfer. I finally did receive word that I was required in the Senior Nurse's office where I was shown a letter saying that the transfer date would be 5 September 1999, only one week away. I was delighted. I telephoned Sara and told her the news, and she too was delighted and suggested that on leaving St Michael's I should buy some presents for the nurses. She would collect me one afternoon and we could go shopping for the presents. Sara amended the present list and they were all neatly gift wrapped. I was very happy to be leaving and probably showed this to everyone. My suitcases were finally packed and I was ready for the day to come around.

Pass the parcel was not a game for me, especially giving out presents and bidding everyone farewell. Simon and Geoffrey had decided to split my journey to Liverpool between them. Simon drove me from St Michael's Hospital to Geoffrey's house, then Geoffrey, Lynne, Sophie and Eliza drove me on to the Rathbone Centre. This time I was the 'parcel' but a happy one as I was going back to Liverpool.

On arrival at the Rathbone Centre, Geoffrey helped with the luggage and friendly staff greeted us. I was given a guided tour of the facilities and shown my room. I was rather surprised at the size of the room, unlike the one at St Michael's, for I had my own room and an en-suite bathroom. I had a comfortable armchair, a table and chairs, and a television, along with a bed, wardrobe and chest of draws. The table was very welcome because I could write letters with more ease. Since being in hospital, I had begun to write many letters to both family and friends, and it became a way of filling up my time.

Having only visited the Rathbone Centre once before my transfer, I did not realise that the unit was near to the shops in the Old Swan area of Liverpool. The staff did not wear uniforms but wore everyday clothes and were very friendly. With it being a brain injury centre, they were obviously more aware and understanding of the type of injuries associated with the head and brain.

My time at the Rathbone Centre continued. I was given a timetable of events for each day. This enabled me to see exactly what I was doing and when I was doing it. The rules were also similar to St Michael's. I was not allowed to leave the centre or go anywhere without permission. This did not perturb me as I had been used to that. There was a television lounge so I could choose whether I watch television or I could go to my room and listen to the radio or watch television alone. During my early days at the Rathbone Centre, my meals were served along with everyone else in the dining room. After I had been there a month or so, I joined the Community Re-entry Programme. It would prepare me to re-enter the community and get me ready to return to my house.

The programme involved discussions on brain injuries and memory loss and the ways in which by use of diaries and other methods I could assist myself. I enjoyed the stimulation and meeting with other people in similar situations to my own. As a group, we got on well together. We attended lectures, which were often interesting, and also attention process training, which was designed to improve concentration. We also had to attend and work with the gardening group. This was where the hospital gardener gave us instructions and gardening advice and once a week we were taken to the centre of Liverpool where we worked for a company keeping their gardens tidy. I enjoyed working away from the hospital environment and got on well with the gardener, even though it was hard work and our rewards were cups of tea or coffee.

The philosophy at the Rathbone Centre was that all work and no play was not good for anyone, so we had social outings regularly. On one occasion, all the patients were taken ten-pin bowling at the local bowling centre. None of us proved particularly skilful, but it was enjoyable nevertheless, and small but friendly rivalries developed. We had full days and our time passed quickly. After several weeks of 'being a good patient', I was given the task of going out to the local shops to buy food. I was responsible for ensuring it was correctly labelled and put away in the fridge or freezer, which finally led to me cooking my own food under close supervision. Once the staff was sure I could cook safely on my own, I was allowed to do this along with preparing the menus. The menus were checked by the staff to ensure that I had a nutritionally good and balanced diet. This was one of the many processes getting me back to learning how to look after myself and all part of the rehabilitation programme.

I was asked to go out to fetch the daily papers for our unit. I must have been the oldest paperboy in the country! I went out each morning and got the papers along with a receipt, upon which I was refunded the money.

The final part of our Community Re-entry Course meant that I, being the last person, was asked to give a talk on a selected topic. As we were fast approaching Christmas, I chose alcohol and drugs and the effect they have on the brain. I got a reasonable response from the audience. The staff later took everyone on the course out to a local pub/restaurant where we all had a meal and a drink together. We each received our certificates to show that we had successfully completed the course.

The year was drawing to a close, I was told that the unit would be holding a dance and having a singer. The time came around and I was very much looking forward to it. We only had soft drinks, but nevertheless the atmosphere was brilliant and really made the evening. I was so enjoying it that I found myself singing along with the songs I knew. I was surprised to hear people in the audience shouting my name: 'Peter give us a song.' I had to look around and, sure enough, fingers were pointing at me. I had not sung with a microphone since being a child. I climbed on the stage. The singer was great and she asked me what I would like to sing, and said that if I was unsure of the words, she would help me by joining in. So, Patsy Cline's 'Crazy' got the worst rendition from me. The singer kindly said, 'Thank you Peter, you will have started something off now. You watch I will get more volunteers now.' She was, of course, right as more volunteers mounted the stage to perform their songs. After the show I felt drained and a little drunk from the atmosphere, not the water that I was drinking!

You loose track of time in hospital. I was therefore given the task of changing the date boards each morning and there were several boards to change, if I remember correctly. The date was fairly clear in my mind; we were well into December, not far off from Christmas, when my son Geoffrey telephoned me to invite me to share Christmas with him and his family in Derby.

I enjoyed my Christmas but from memory I was very quiet

and took a book with me, which I spent most of the holiday reading. In all probability, I may have spoilt their Christmas, as it is a time for families. Sophie and Eliza, my grand-daughters, enjoyed the Christmas period and had a wonderful time, which is only natural for children. Lynne's family also joined us, so the house was full and bustling with Christmas spirit.

Simon, Sara, James and their new baby Jonathan arrived on Boxing Day morning to collect me and take me back to Liverpool. We spent a couple of days at my house. Sara cooked a meal on Boxing Day, whilst I attempted to make the house look a little more Christmas-like, although I was not a successful as Pat would have liked. To me it was joyful to be back in my own house with my family. Time flew by and it was time to return to the Rathbone.

Whilst still at Rathbone Hospital I was now almost a trustee patient, and in January I was being allowed home for the odd day, which soon progressed to a weekend. At first, it was wonderful being back in my house, but the house seemed deserted and lonely. I missed Pat so very much. Looking back, I realise why the doctors had suggested that I need not try hypnosis in an attempt to recall some of my lost memory due to me not being able to sleep at night. Not remembering anything of the accident, I was sleeping very well. Doctors are very clever and experienced people, but I am a great believer in the philosophy that God only helps those who help themselves. Therefore, I began to write to a Heart to Heart column in the local newspaper, the *Liverpool Echo*. I was hoping to meet ladies for friendship.

At one of the review meetings organised at the Rathbone, they recommended and suggested that if and when I was released to live back at home on a permanent basis, that I would need support people. Their advice was taken and I now received care from a private care organisation. The hospital also recommended that I join or become a member of a voluntary organisation, and again I followed their advice and became a voluntary worker for Age Concern. I worked for several months at an Age Concern lunch club until the site's closure. I assisted in serving drinks, tea and coffee, helping with the washing and drying of the crockery, and in the serving of meals. I enjoyed the work and everyone called me by my first name. Before the lunch club closed, however, the organiser asked me if I would write an article for the Age Concern monthly journal, the *Grapevine*. I did this and it was printed.

One day my son Geoffrey and his family called to visit. At the same time, I also received a visit from Bill, an old colleague of mine when I worked at Otis Elevators. I had sent a letter to his London office along with a copy of the article I had written for Age Concern. Bill invited me to meet more old colleagues in the London office, and a few days after Bill's visit I received a formal letter inviting me to visit London. I replied accepting their invitation and travel arrangements were made. The headquarters in London were all new and very nice. Many senior people including the Information & Systems Director greeted me. It really was like all our yesterdays. At the end of the visit, Bill drove me back to the train station. It was a very enjoyable and memorable day.

A few days later – or maybe it was a few weeks later – one of my care support workers pointed out to me an advert in our local papers. A few weeks earlier I had been rejected in no uncertain terms by a lady whom, I thought, was on the same perfect wavelength and would bring me long-term happiness. I trier I am, and on reading the advert and completing my application, I joined a dating agency. Once you have become a member, they send you details of their female members that suit your profile. If you choose, it allows you to meet women who might be a perfect match. At the very least, you know their age and interests, and you have a brief summary of their personality.

I have met several nice ladies through this organisation Perfect Harmony, and owing to my accident the hospital had written to me to say that I will never be able to drive again, so I have to use public transport unless they live within walking distance from my house. Fortunately, I met a lady through the organisation. We have met several times over three months and have been on several coach trips together. Because of my accident, I am now very impulsive, which this woman is well aware of. If you hide anything from a woman, it is not long before she finds out! It will indeed be wonderful if I am lucky enough not to say the wrong thing to the lady that will destroy our relationship.

I cannot guarantee anything these days because I think one thing and say what I do not want to say, so we will see what happens. Maybe this time someone up there will say, 'Hold on, he had been punished enough.' In the last few months, I have again been fortunate to meet several times with two wonderful women. One of these I have fallen in love with. I never thought that it would occur to me again, she has everything that I could only dream about. She has a heart of gold and has told me often that she loves me. I now know that I love her. We like the same things, music, quiet places, in fact everything. This time I am sure that we will soon have

*My fiancée,
Margaret Ashton,
and I by the
Eiffel Tower, Paris,
Sunday, 15 April
2001.*

a long-lasting and permanent relationship. We have been recently on a coach holiday for four days to Paris, which is a wonderful and romantic city. And, as the song says, spring time in Paris was lovely. It is a most beautiful city. There is so much to marvel at that we were fortunate to have a French guide for our visit to the Palace of Versailles. We learnt so much and received a history lesson and were enthralled at our guide's knowledge of everything we were shown. My schoolboy French learnt more than forty years ago came back to me; I was not very fluent, but was able to say basic words such as thank you, please, good night and so on. A visit to Paris is not complete unless one visits the Eiffel Tower. It was a dull day with rain about, but Margaret, for that is her name, seeing my enthusiasm made us join the long queue and within twenty minutes we were speeding up the tower in the lift. We got out of the lift at the middle level. Walking round the tower and looking down I suddenly felt quite dizzy. I had to hold on to the rail. I have never been so frightened! Worse was to come because we could not find the lift to take us down, so we descended the metal stairs. To concentrate my mind I counted the steps and when I reached two hundred I gave up counting. We reached the lower level and had a pleasant surprise as there was a restaurant and Margaret joined the small queue and returned soon with a full tray with coffee and food. It really cemented my love for her as the food and drink tasted delicious. The views from the tower, even at the lower level, were magnificent, with the whole of Paris spread out below.

Our holiday flashed by and it was an unforgettable time. Then it was the long journey home by coach. Margaret and I are even talking about buying a bungalow together to begin our long-term relationship as a completely married couple. We have now fixed the date and time for our wedding. I never thought that I could be so happy again as I am now.